A Practical Guide to HEALTH FOODS

Recognizing, preparing and cooking natural foods

Pamela Westland

Columbus Books
London

BY THE SAME AUTHOR

The High-Fibre Cookbook, Martin Dunitz
The 60-Minute Cookbook, Faber
One-pot Cooking, Fontana
The Everyday Gourmet, Granada
Bean Feast, Granada
Food for Keeps, Granada
The Complete Grill Cookbook, Granada
High-Fibre Vegetarian Cookery, Granada
Encyclopedia of Spices, Marshall Cavendish
The Hostess Cookbook, with Anne Ager, Octopus
A Taste of the Country, Penguin
The Busy Cook's Book, St Michael

Note American equivalents for both quantities and names of certain ingredients appear throughout this book as the final items listed.

Copyright © 1984 Pamela Westland

First published in 1984 by
Columbus Books
Devonshire House, 29 Elmfield Road, Bromley, Kent BR1 1LT

Designed by Astrid

British Library Cataloguing in Publication Data

Westland, Pamela
   A practical guide to health foods.
   1. Cookery (Natural foods)
   I. Title
   641.5'637   TX 741

   ISBN 0-86287-091-7

Printed and bound in Yugoslavia

CONTENTS

Introduction   4

Dried fruits   8

Nuts and seeds   26

Pulses   42

Grains   58

Pasta   72

Drinks   78

Dairy produce   84

Vegetable products   94

Flavourings   98

Herbs and spices   101

Fats and oils   103

Sweeteners   105

Salt   109

Glossary   113

Recipe index   127

INTRODUCTION

Every one of us who regularly goes into health-food stores or chooses items from the 'natural food' counters in supermarkets is part of a growing wholefood revolution; and it is very exciting. It can also be a little bewildering. Some of the health foods seem so familiar that it is difficult to see what is so special about them, and why they have suddenly become important. Others look so totally unfamiliar that it takes a fair bit of imagination to visualize them being turned into a tasty lunch for the family.

That is where I hope this book will help. Look on it as a guided tour of the health-food shelves, and I hope you will find that you can feed the family and entertain your friends more healthily, more deliciously and certainly no more expensively than ever before.

For easy reference the book is divided into sections. It takes each range of health foods, each store classification, and puts it under the microscope — dried fruits, nuts and seeds, pulses, grains, pasta, drinks, dairy produce, dried vegetables, flavourings, fats and sweeteners. You will find all kinds of background details about where and how the foods are grown, how they are prepared and processed, how to recognize them, prepare and cook them. There are details of the nutrients and dietary fibre content and of the advantages and drawbacks of various food items. (Even health foods can be packed with calories, and some are secret purveyors of unwanted fat.) The recipes that follow represent a range of dishes for which you can use these foods, in meals that will take you right through from breakfast to supper.

The beautiful watercolour paintings that illustrate all the recipe sections show you far better than words can what both the ingredients and the finished dishes look like.

Did you know, for example, that brazil nuts grow tightly packed together inside a shell about the size of a coconut; that hazelnuts contain over 40 per cent water and are lower in both calories and dietary fibre than most other nuts; that the fat in coconut sets every bit as hard at room temperature as a block of butter, and is every bit as cholesterol-packed? Turn to the illustrated section on nuts and seeds and you will find this information at your fingertips.

Last, but by no means least, there is a glossary of health-food ingredients and related terms.

Health foods have been the subject of ever-growing discussion for years now, attitudes have changed radically and knowledge is constantly being increased as new medical evidence emerges. What we eat is a vital issue to all of us. I hope this book will help you to take full advantage of our new-found awareness and of the exciting possibilities of the 'new' foods now available to us all.

It was the Industrial Revolution that did it. A century or so ago it changed the whole character of our food. Once it became possible to mill grains to a novel whiteness, produce a flour with ever-higher raising properties, and produce food with a new lightness, they became a way of life. Thus we discarded much of the natural goodness in our everyday food.

A slow but determined revolution has caused us to understand the error of our ways. At last, now, we realize that without thinking or even caring for all these years we have been frittering away the nutrients and fibre in our foods and putting our health at risk.

At last, because of the increasing publicity given to medical findings and to increased media discussion, it is not just cranks who go into health-food shops, meticulously read the labels on everything they buy and go home to try out recipes using whole grains, pulses, nuts and seeds. We are all doing it!

I see the health-food scene as breaking down into four separate but closely related issues. The first is the need for dietary fibre, which has certainly had its share of publicity over the past few years. That can be summed up in terms of whole grains, fruit and vegetables. Second is the question of fats and oils, and the confusing comparison between the relative merits and demerits of polyunsaturates, mono-unsaturates and saturated fatty acids; also, the stark realization that we consume too much of all of them. Third is the guilt-ridden subject of sweeteners: the case of raw, natural sugar as against refined white sugar; the case for honey; and the very good case for leaving them all alone as far as possible! And now another discussion is entering the arena: item four, the question of salt, that age-old natural flavouring, which is currently getting very bad marks from medical experts.

Take the case for dietary fibre for a start. Recent research has shown that a substantially increased intake of dietary fibre is vital to our well-being. In the Western world our average daily intake stands at only about 20 grams, whilst experts now recommend that it should be much nearer 30–35 grams. Food which has a high fibre content, and contains plenty of bulk, is quickly and easily transported through the digestive system. As it travels through the digestive tract it takes up liquid like a sponge and considerably increases in bulk. The digestive juices have to penetrate the fibre to extract the nutrients surrounding it, and these are slowly and steadily passed into the bloodstream. Without the fibre, the food waste lingers in the intestine and the nutrients are released too quickly, necessitating the release of large amounts of insulin to digest them. Lack of fibre can lead to coronary heart disease, cancer of the large bowel, diverticular disease of the colon and others besides.

Dietary fibre is present only in plant foods, the supportive structure of all cereals, fruit and vegetables, the woody tissues and the cellulose and gums which bind them together. This is the very part of the grain that is milled out to produce white flour, when some 28 per cent of the germ and bran is frittered away — some of it to be sold back to us in packets on the health-food counter. This is the ingredient we lack if we choose white polished rice in preference to brown rice, and 'ordinary' pasta in preference to wholewheat kinds, made from the whole grain of hard durum wheat.

Because we need to increase our daily intake of dietary fibre so dramatically, it is important to recognize the foods that supply it in worthwhile amounts. Dried fruits have roughly ten times the amount of fibre carried in their fresh counterparts. A huge 100-gram (4-ounce) apple, complete with the skin, contains about 2 grams of fibre. Chop dried fruits into your muesli, add them to fresh fruits in a pie or compote, choose them instead of salted snacks to nibble, and weight for weight you have increased your daily fibre intake ten times.

The section on pulses, with recipes for soups, salads, casseroles, vegetable accompaniments, Indian-inspired dishes and pies and pasties, is of immense importance in the fibre story. Pulses of all kinds, from split orange lentils to jet-black beans, are packed with dietary fibre — essential proteins too, of course — and represent one of the most concentrated ways of increasing the fibre intake.

Nuts and seeds, those tiny power-packed capsules representing the next generation of the plant, are also high up the fibre table. If you ate 100 grams (4 ounces) of shelled almonds you would clock up 14.3 grams of fibre — but also, unfortunately, 670 calories and 53.5 grams of fat.

For our health's sake, we should drastically reduce our consumption of all fats, but specifically of those which set hard at room temperature — butter, lard, suet, hard margarine and coconut oil, the saturated fatty acids. These are the ones held responsible for the increase in the amount of cholesterol, a waxy, fat-like substance in the bloodstream and, in turn, for blockage of the arteries. It is easy to recognize fat in the form of butter or margarine, less easy to realize it in full-fat milk, cream, full-fat cheeses and yoghurt. Changing to low-fat yoghurt, choosing cottage cheese in place of hard cheese for some dishes, using sunflower or safflower oil, for example, which are high in the less harmful polyunsaturated fats, and sunflower margarine in place of the hard type, would help cut down your fat intake.

In the case of fats, as in the case of sweeteners, the conclusion has to be that only a very little of what you fancy does you good. And any more can be positively harmful. I always use natural raw sugars, the kind which state the country of origin — those sun-drenched Caribbean islands — in preference to refined sugars with a list of ingredients on the packet. Sugar is a natural food and should not have 'ingredients', but unnatural brown sugars do. Look carefully at the labels — the watchword of so many sections of this book — and you will realize that brown sugar, like brown bread, can be made up of the refined white product, but coloured.

Honey is another case for moderation: a glance at the calorie count shows it up for what it is — just another sweetener and completely lacking in dietary fibre. For that reason, I choose dried fruits whenever possible for the dual role they play. A few dates chopped into muesli are far sweeter than a spoonful of sugar, yet they add fibre as well. A handful of raisins stirred into bread dough adds flavour beyond just sweetness.

Then there is salt. The human body actually needs less than 0.5 gram salt per day, yet what we shake on to our plates and consume in our foods mounts up to an astonishing 12 grams per person (UK statistics). Excesses of sodium, which makes up 40 per cent of the weight of salt, can contribute to hypertension, heart disease and brain haemorrhage: a very good reason for checking the labels on pre-packed, canned and processed foods, many of which (even the so-called sweet products) contain it. Watch out for sodium in its other forms too — as sodium sorbate, sodium benzoate, sodium sulphate, sodium hydrogen sulphite and many more besides, which are often listed in the small print. Once you get into the habit of increasing other flavourings in the foods you cook, herbs and spices especially, the absence of the salt shaker will assume less importance.

As you go through the book you will find pointers to the essential vitamins, minerals and dietary fibre elements in the whole range of health foods, with ideas of how to mix and match them for everyday family meals and party pieces. The important thing to understand is that even 'health foods' — dried fruits, nuts, dairy produce and so on — are only healthy in moderation. It is a tricky balance that I very much hope this book will help you to achieve.

Pamela Westland

DRIED FRUITS

For thousands of years fruit has been preserved by drying in the heat of the sun, either in direct sunlight or – in the case of figs and dates – by burying in the hot sand. By drawing out the moisture the drying process inhibits bacterial growth. Increasingly, now, fruit is dried by controlled heat in the form of hot air streams or in ovens, or freeze-drying. By this process the fruit is first frozen, then transferred to vacuum chambers where the ice crystals vaporize, leaving the fruit with a moisture content which can be as low as 2 per cent. To preserve the colour of apricots, peaches and sultanas producers are allowed to add a small amount of sulphur dioxide, a chemical which disperses on exposure to air, water and heat. Dried fruits are a rich source of sugar, in the form of glucose, and of vitamins, salts and minerals. Currants, raisins and sultanas, the vine fruits, are the dried produce of different varieties of grape. Of the tree fruits, apples, apricots, bananas, dates, figs, mulberries, peaches, pears and prunes are dried commercially. Store dried fruits in a cool, airy place and, once packets have been opened, in airtight containers.

Macerated fruits

1 kg (2¼ lb) (7 cups) mixed dried fruits
  (apple rings, apricots, peaches, pears,
  prunes)
75 g (3 oz) (¾ cup) pine nuts
75 g (3 oz) (¾ cup) blanched, slivered
  almonds
30 ml (2 tablespoons) orange-flower water
30 ml (2 tablespoons) rosewater
strips of thinly pared orange rind

In preserving jars, make layers of the fruits and nuts, sprinkling the orange-flower water and rosewater between each layer. Push a strip of orange rind into each jar and pour on water to cover. Close the jars and leave the fruit in a light place to macerate for at least 6 days, topping up the water as needed. Serve with plain yoghurt or soured cream.

For a long-keeping preserve, put on the lids without closing tightly. Stand the jars on a trivet in a pan with water up the necks. Bring to the boil and simmer for 20 minutes. Cool, close the lids, label and store in a cool, dry, dark place.

Fills 3 500-g (1-lb) preserving jars

Mixed tree fruits

The flavours, colours and textures of dried tree fruits complement each other so well that it is sometimes convenient to buy them in a mixed pack. Mixtures include apple rings, apricots, peaches, pears and prunes; figs are sometimes added but with their dominant flavour are not suitable for all dishes. To cook the fruits, soak them in water or fruit juice for several hours. Poach them in the soaking liquid, with added sugar and spices if you wish, for 20–30 minutes, or bake them under a scone or crumble topping. Drain cooked fruits for a double-crust pie filling, or arrange them to fill or decorate a flan case. Liquidize the mixed fruits to make a delicious purée – an unusual spread for sponge sandwich cakes and a refreshingly different base for fruit fools, ice cream, soufflés, mousses and sweet sauces.

Dried fruit compote

500 g (1 lb) (3 cups) mixed dried fruits
  (apple rings, apricots, figs, peaches,
  pears, prunes)
50 g (2 oz) (⅓ cup) seedless raisins
1 lemon
1 orange
30 ml (2 tablespoons) light muscovado/
  brown sugar
50 g (2 oz) (½ cup) pistachios

Soak the mixed fruits and raisins in a casserole in 700 ml (1¼ pints) (3 cups) water for about 2 hours. Grate the rind and squeeze the juice of the lemon and orange. Add the lemon rind and juice to the fruit, cover the casserole and cook in the oven at 180°C, 350°F, Gas 4 for 1¼ hours. Strain off the juice, add the orange rind and juice and the sugar, and stir over low heat to dissolve. Bring to the boil and simmer for 5 minutes. Pour over fruit and cool. Stir in the pistachios and serve with plain yoghurt or soured cream.

Serves 6

Apples

One of the few fruits to retain all their vitamin C content in the drying process, dried apples are sold as creamy-white rings of the peeled and cored fruit, and as freeze-dried flakes. Add the dry rings to casseroles of pork or bacon or chop them into poultry stuffings or breakfast muesli. Dip soaked apple rings in batter for sweet fritters or grill them to serve with yoghurt as a simple dessert, or with pork chops as a garnish. The reconstituted flakes are useful for apple sauce or, with blackberries for added fibre, as a pie filling.

Apricots

Dried apricots have a much stronger – and some say more delicious – flavour than their fresh counterparts. They have a higher protein content than any other dried fruit and contain 12 mg vitamin C per 100 g (4 oz). They are exported mainly by Australia, South Africa and Turkey and are available whole, halved or in pieces. Turkish wild apricots, small and dark bronze, are even sweeter. Lamb and chicken dishes sweetened with dried apricots are a feature of North African cuisine. Mixed with honey and mustard, the fruit purée makes a golden glaze for baked ham and poultry. Whole apricots soaked in orange juice are a tasty addition to fresh fruit salads.

Apple rings in apricot sauce

250 g (8 oz) (1½ cups) dried apricots,
  soaked
½ lemon
250 g (8 oz) (2⅔ cups) dried apple rings,
  soaked and drained
30 ml (2 tablespoons) apricot liqueur
50 g (2 oz) (½ cup) blanched almonds
50 g (2 oz) (⅓ cup) seedless raisins

Cook the apricots in the soaking water with the thinly pared lemon peel for 20 minutes. Strain off the liquid, add the lemon and poach the apple rings for 10 minutes – do not allow them to collapse. Arrange the apple rings in a serving dish. Liquidize the apricots with 125 ml (4 fl oz) (½ cup) of the liquid and the liqueur. Pour over the fruit and cool. Scatter with the almonds and raisins and serve chilled.

Serves 4

Apricot mousse

250 g (8 oz) (1½ cups) dried apricots,
  soaked
15 ml (1 tablespoon) agar-agar
45 ml (3 tablespoons) orange juice
3 large eggs
50 g (2 oz) (¼ cup) light muscovado/
  brown sugar
150 ml (¼ pint) (⅔ cup) double/heavy
  cream
150 ml (¼ pint) (⅔ cup) plain yoghurt
apricot paste 'flowers' (see below) to
  decorate

Cook the apricots in a little of the soaking liquid for 20 minutes, then liquidize. Soak the agar-agar in the orange juice, bring to the boil and stir into the apricot purée. Cool. Beat the egg yolks and sugar until light. Beat together the cream and yoghurt. Stir the egg and the cream mixtures into the purée. Chill for 15 minutes. Stiffly whisk the egg whites and fold them in. Divide the mixtures between 4 individual glasses and chill for at least 1 hour. Decorate with 'flowers' of apricot paste.

Apricot paste

100 g (4 oz) (1 cup) blanched almonds
250 g (8 oz) (1½ cups) dried apricots
30 ml (2 tablespoons) light muscovado/
  brown sugar

Grind the almonds in a food processor or blender until they are like fine powder. Add the apricots and sugar and process to form a paste. Knead the paste until smooth. To store, wrap in clingfilm/plastic wrap and keep in a covered container.

Sprinkle a board lightly with ground almonds and roll out the paste. Cut it into shapes and use to decorate mousses, fruits creams and cakes.

For a simple petit-four, shape the paste into walnut-sized balls, roll in ground almonds and push in a toasted almond.

Peaches

Unlike apricots, peaches lose flavour in the drying process. Remedy this by soaking and cooking them in orange or apple juice, perhaps with a little white wine or sherry added. Add the fruit to chicken casseroles or, for unusual kebabs, thread soaked peach halves on skewers with marinated cubes of chicken wrapped in bacon. Poach soaked peaches in a sauce of raspberries liquidized with sugar and lemon juice, or sandwich cooked peach halves with apricot paste (page 11) and top them with yoghurt. Containing about 7 mg per 100 g (4 oz) of fruit, dried peaches are a good source of iron.

Prunes

The USA is one of the leading exporters of prunes, the dried product of extra-sweet varieties of plum taken with them by early immigrants from Europe. Lower in calories than most other dried fruits, prunes are sold whole both with and without the stones, canned in syrup, packaged in the form of freeze-dried flakes – rather like powdered chocolate – and as canned juice, popular in the USA. The dried fruit can be eaten 'raw', stoned and filled with soft cheese, almond paste or whole almonds. Prune stuffing complements roast duck and goose, and a few prunes make a tasty addition to pork and beef casseroles. The flakes are good stirred into muesli and in cake mixtures.

Peach reveille

250 g (8 oz) (1½ cups) dried peaches
300 ml (½ pint) (1¼ cups) unsweetened
   orange juice
½ stick cinnamon
600 ml (1 pint) (2½ cups) plain yoghurt

Soak the peaches in the orange juice, then cook them with the cinnamon stick and a very little added water for 20 minutes. Cool. Remove 2 peach halves and chop them finely. Remove the cinnamon. Liquidize the peaches, cooking liquid and yoghurt and stir in the chopped peaches. Serve chilled.

Serves 4

Prune dominoes

12 large prunes, stoned
75 g (3 oz) (1/3 cup) yoghurt cheese
  (page 85)
12 blanched almonds, toasted

Fill the prunes with the yoghurt cheese, piling it up to make a 'dome'. Just before serving, push a toasted almond into each prune (the almonds will soften if added in advance). Serve as a cocktail snack on sticks.

Serves 4–6

Devils on horseback

16 large prunes, stoned
16 blanched almonds
8 rashers streaky bacon, rind removed

Fill each prune with an almond. Cut the bacon rashers in half and stretch each piece by 'stroking' it firmly with the back of a knife. Wrap each prune in bacon and thread on to skewers. Cook under a medium grill for 4–5 minutes, turning the skewers frequently. Serve hot, as a cocktail snack or as an accompaniment to a pilaff or risotto.

Serves 4

Sultanas

Britain's most popular dried vine fruits, sultanas are dried from small, white seedless grapes produced in the United States, Turkey, Greece, Australia and South Africa. A small quantity of sulphur dioxide may be added to preserve the attractive light amber colour, and a fine film of oil sprayed on to the fruit to keep each one separate. To remove these additives soak the sultanas in water, or buy 'natural' fruits in health-food shops. Most dried vine fruits are sold washed, dried and ready to use. If you buy unwashed fruit, wash it in a colander under running water and drain it thoroughly. To use it for baking – when damp fruit would sink – pat it with kitchen paper to dry and then toss it in a little of the flour specified in the recipe.

Sultanas, raisins and currants are an important source of vitamins, especially vitamin B, and minerals, notably iron and potassium. They contain only about two-thirds as many calories as the equivalent weight of sugar, and are a good source of dietary fibre. Sultanas have 7 per cent, raisins 6.8 and currants 8.7 per cent fibre.

Potato and sultana salad

500 g (1 lb) potatoes, cooked, peeled and
  thickly diced
100 g (4 oz) (²/₃ cup) sultanas
30 ml (2 tablespoons) snipped chives
2 shallots, thinly sliced into rings
½ orange
150 ml (¼ pint) (²/₃ cup) plain yoghurt
45 ml (3 tablespoons) mayonnaise
1 hard-boiled egg, finely chopped
salt and freshly ground black pepper

Mix together the potatoes, sultanas, chives
and shallots. Very thinly pare the orange
and cut off any white pith that comes away
with the rind. Chop the rind very finely and
mix with the vegetables. Squeeze the orange
juice and mix it with the yoghurt,
mayonnaise and chopped egg. Season the
dressing with salt and pepper and pour over
the salad. Mix thoroughly. Serve chilled.

Serves 4–6

Baked New York cheesecake

150 g (6 oz) (1 cup) wholewheat flour
a pinch of salt
75 g (3 oz) (⅓ cup) margarine
1 egg yolk, beaten
  FILLING:
  50 g (2 oz) (¼ cup) butter
  25 g (1 oz) (2 tablespoons) light
    muscovado/brown sugar
  15 ml (1 tablespoon) wholewheat flour
  350 g (12 oz) (1½ cups) curd cheese
  30 ml (2 tablespoons) double/heavy
    cream
  2 eggs, separated
  grated rind and juice of 1 orange
  grated rind and juice of 1 lemon
  100 g (4 oz) (²/₃ cup) sultanas
1 egg white for brushing

To make the pastry, mix together the flour
and salt, rub in the margarine and bind with
the beaten egg yolks. Roll out on a lightly
floured board and line a greased 20-cm
(8-inch) flan ring on a baking sheet. Cut the
trimming into 6-mm (¼-inch) strips.

Cream together the butter and sugar and
beat in the flour, cheese, cream and egg
yolks, then the orange and lemon rind and
juice and the sultanas. Whisk the egg whites
until stiff, then fold into the mixture.

Pour the cheesecake filling on to the
pastry base and level the top. Make a lattice
pattern with the pastry strips. Brush the top
with egg white. Bake in the oven at 180 °C,
350 °F, Gas 4 for 1 hour, or until the top is
golden brown. Leave to cool in the tin. Serve
chilled, with cinnamon-flavoured whipped
cream.

Serves 8

Currants

Since classical times currants have been produced in Greece from the small black grapes grown along the Gulf of Corinth – their name is a corruption of this original area of cultivation – and for centuries they were known as Corinth raisins. Today, they are also exported by Australia. Small, almost jet black and shrivelled, currants are less attractive in appearance and less sweet in flavour than sultanas and raisins, though the sugar content, at around 64 per cent, varies little between the three vine fruits. They are not as widely used 'raw' as other dried-grape products – as a snack, in salads or muesli, for example. Currants come into their own in baked goods and steamed puddings and many regional and traditional favourites feature them at their best – Dundee cake, Eccles cakes, Christmas cake, Christmas pudding and steamed suet pudding among them. They combine well with lemon, as demonstrated by the Hungarian-style pancakes shown below.

Hungarian-style pancakes

125 g (4 oz) (2/3 cup) wholewheat flour
salt
2 eggs
300 ml (1/2 pint) (1 1/4 cups) milk
15 ml (1 tablespoon) melted butter
15 ml (1 tablespoon) light muscovado/
*   brown sugar*
lemon twists to decorate
oil for frying
*   FILLING:*
*   250 g (8 oz) (1 cup) cottage cheese,*
*   sieved*
*   75 g (3 oz) (1/2 cup) currants*
*   grated rind and juice of 1 lemon*
*   sugar (optional)*
*   SAUCE:*
*   150 ml (1/4 pint) (2/3 cup) soured*
*   cream*
*   150 ml (1/4 pint) (2/3 cup) plain*
*   yoghurt*
*   grated rind and juice of 1 orange*

Mix together the flour and salt, make a well in the centre and add the eggs and a little milk. Stir to mix well, then beat until smooth. Beat in the rest of the milk, then the melted butter and sugar.

Lightly grease a small frying-pan. When it is hot, pour in just enough batter to cover the base thinly. Cook over moderate/high heat until the mixture has set and the underside is brown. Flip or toss the pancake and cook the other side. Slide it on to a heated plate and keep it warm while you cook the remaining batter.

To make the filling, stir 30 ml (2 tablespoons) of the soured cream (from the sauce) into the cottage cheese. Stir in the currants, the grated lemon rind and lemon juice and a little sugar if you wish.

Spread the filling over the pancakes. Fold them in half and then in half again, to make quarter-circle shapes. Keep them warm.

Beat the remaining soured cream with the yoghurt, orange rind and juice and serve the sauce separately.

Serves 4

16

Variations

Other dried fruits make delicious pancake fillings. Try apricot purée mixed with finely chopped dates and a squeeze of lemon juice, or a purée of mixed 'tree' fruits with seedless raisins, lightly spiced with orange rind and ground cinnamon.

Celebration cake

250 g (8 oz) (1 cup) butter
250 g (8 oz) (1 cup) dark muscovado/ brown sugar
6 eggs, separated
75 ml (5 tablespoons) (1/3 cup) molasses
grated rind and juice of 1 orange
350 g (12 oz) (2 1/4 cups) wholewheat flour
5 ml (1 teaspoon) ground cinnamon
5 ml (1 teaspoon) ground ginger
2.5 ml (1/2 teaspoon) grated nutmeg
2.5 ml (1/2 teaspoon) ground allspice
5 ml (1 teaspoon) salt
5 ml (1 teaspoon) bicarbonate of soda
350 g (12 oz) (2 cups) currants
350 g (12 oz) (2 cups) seedless raisins
250 g (8 oz) (1 1/3 cups) sultanas
125 g (4 oz) (3/4 cup) candied orange peel, finely chopped
300 ml (1/2 pint) (1 1/4 cups) milk
90 ml (6 tablespoons) (1/3 cup) brandy
40 g (1 1/2 oz) (1/2 cup) blanched almonds, halved

Grease a 23-cm (9-inch) cake-tin. Line the base and sides with 2 thicknesses of grease-proof paper, and grease thoroughly.

In a large mixing bowl, beat together the butter and sugar, then beat in the egg yolks one at a time. Beat in the molasses, orange rind and juice. Sift together the flour, spices, salt and soda. Mix together the dried fruits and the peel. Stir together the milk and brandy.

Gradually add to the sugar mixtures the flour and spices, the fruits and the liquid, beating between each addition. Stiffly whisk the egg whites and fold them into the mixture.

Turn the mixture into the tin, level the top and press a slight hollow in the centre, so that the cake will be flat when it rises. Arrange the almonds in a pattern on top.

Bake in the oven at 140 °C, 275 °F, Gas 1½ for 2½–3 hours, or until the cake is evenly cooked. To test, push a skewer into the centre. It should come out clean. If the cake becomes too brown, cover the top with foil.

Cool the cake in the tin, then turn it out, peel off the paper and leave on a wire rack to become completely cold. Wrap in a double thickness of foil and store in an airtight tin. The cake should keep fresh for several months.

Makes one 23-cm (9-inch) cake

Raisins

Whether the grapes are left to dry on the vine or spread out in the heat of the sun, raisins capture the very essence of sunshine. The purplish-black dessert raisins called muscatels are dried Muscat grapes, grown in the Malaga region of Spain, in Australia and South Africa. Because of their pips, they are rarely used in cooking. If you do wish to seed them, soak them first, then hold each one between thumb and forefinger and rub gently – it's a slow job! Seedless raisins, from California, South Africa, Iran and Afghanistan, are dried from seedless grapes and more suitable for cooking. Size depends on the variety of grape. To chop large ones, snip them with kitchen scissors. Raisins should be plump, shiny and moist. If they have become too dry – or simply to add flavour – soak them in fruit juice, wine, spirit or, for cakes and teabreads, in tea or coffee. Raisin sauce, in which the fruit is simmered with honey and lemon juice, makes a good accompaniment to baked ham, roast pork, steamed puddings and, hot or cold, to ice cream. Snapdragons, a dish of raisins flamed in brandy, is traditional at Hallowe'en, and in Finland a purée of raisins soaked in spirit is served with porridge.

Skewered meatballs

500 g (1 lb) lean leg of lamb, finely
  minced
30 ml (2 tablespoons) potato flour
1 clove garlic, crushed
1 egg
15 ml (1 tablespoon) chopped parsley
2.5 ml (½ teaspoon) ground cumin
salt and pepper
oil, for frying
  SAUCE:
  300 ml (½ pint) (1¼ cups) plain
    yoghurt
  2.5 ml (½ teaspoon) ground cinnamon
  5 ml (1 teaspoon) light
    muscovado/brown sugar

Beat and mash together the lamb, flour and garlic until it makes a moist paste. Beat in the egg, parsley and cumin and season with salt and pepper. Knead the mixture until it is smooth. Shape into rounds slightly smaller than golf balls and mould firmly.

Heat the oil in a frying-pan; when it is hot, fry the lamb balls over moderate heat for 12–15 minutes, turning them frequently to brown evenly. They should be crisp on the outside and moist inside. Thread the meatballs on to skewers and serve with the Turkish pilaff and sauce.

To make the sauce, gently heat the yoghurt, cinnamon and sugar; serve separately. Alternatively, pour the sauce over the meatballs and simmer over very low heat for 5 minutes.

Serves 4

Turkish pilaff

45 ml (3 tablespoons) vegetable oil
1 medium onion, chopped
250 g (8 oz) (1 cup) brown short-grain rice
600 ml (1 pint) (2½ cups) hot vegetable
stock
salt and freshly-ground black pepper
2.5 ml (½ teaspoon) ground cinnamon
125 g (4 oz) (⅔ cup) seedless raisins
1 green pepper, seeded and thinly sliced
75 g (3 oz) (¾ cup) blanched almonds,
toasted

Heat 30 ml (2 tablespoons) of the oil in a pan and fry the onion over moderate heat, stirring frequently, for 3–4 minutes. Add the rice and stir for 1 minute. Pour on the stock, add salt, pepper, cinnamon and raisins, stir and bring to the boil. Cover and simmer over low heat for 35 minutes.

Fry the pepper in the remaining oil, stir into the rice, cover and cook for a further 5 minutes, or until the rice is tender and all the stock absorbed. Stir in the almonds just before serving.

Serves 4

Note *This pilaff can be used to fill green peppers and aubergines/egg plants, or as a stuffing for poultry or pork.*

Muscatels in brandy

When muscatels are steeped in brandy the dried grapes take up the brandy flavour and the spirit takes on the unmistakable muskiness of the fruit.

Wash the muscatels and pick off any stalks. Pack into a screw-topped jar and top up with 'cooking' brandy. Cover and leave in the dark for at least 2 months. Strain, and store the fruit (which will keep indefinitely) and the spirit separately.

Seed the muscatels and add a few to fresh fruit salad, stir them into fruit mousses and ice creams or use them as toppings, or serve them as a luxury sweetmeat with nuts. Drink the flavoured brandy as a liqueur or add it to fruit salads and sauces.

Dates

One of the most ancient of fruits, date palms have been in cultivation for over 5,000 years and are a staple food of the Middle East. Three-quarters of the world's supply comes from Iraq, the remainder from the United States, North Africa and Israel. Dried dates are sold whole, unstoned and still on the stalks in wooden boxes, in tubs, or packets. Stoned dates are compressed into blocks, convenient for chopping. Since dried dates comprise almost two-thirds sugar, they make a good high-fibre substitute and can be ground to a sugary powder.

Figs

Turkey is the main exporter of dried figs (notably the delicious Smyrna variety), which have been cultivated throughout the Mediterranean for thousands of years. Whole figs are packed in decorative boxes as a sweetmeat, the greyish sugary coating a reminder that the dried fruit contains over 50 per cent sugar. For cooking, whole figs are compressed and more economically packaged. Soak them in warm water for several hours, and simmer in fresh water or fruit juice for 20–30 minutes. You can also buy fig paste compressed into shiny, dark-brown blocks and ready to roll out as a cake filling or chop for instant use in muesli, scones, cakes and puddings.

Date 'sugar'

500 g (1 lb) whole dried dates, stoned

Spread out the dates, each one separate, on a baking tray. Bake in the oven at 130 °C, 250 °F, Gas ½ for 10–12 hours, turning occasionally to dry evenly. They should be very hard and completely dry.

Grind the dates a few at a time in a blender or food processor until they are like coarse powder. Store in an airtight tin.

Use as a sugar substitute when cooking fruit, sauces and puddings, and to sprinkle over muesli and yoghurt. A pinch of date 'sugar' is particularly good in salad dressings. To use in baking, stir it into the liquid ingredients and set aside for 10 minutes. This prevents burning.

Makes about 250 g (8 oz) – according to type of dates used

Baked apples with figs

4 large cooking apples, cored
100 g (4 oz) (¼ lb) fig paste, finely
  chopped
grated rind and juice of 1 orange
30 ml (2 tablespoons) pecans, chopped
25 g (1 oz) (2 tablespoons) butter, softened
30 ml (2 tablespoons) light muscovado/
  brown sugar
150 ml (¼ pint) (⅔ cup) clear apple
  juice or water
20 ml (4 teaspoons) lemon juice
30 ml (2 tablespoons) clear honey
100 ml (3½ fl oz) (½ cup) double/heavy
  cream
100 ml (3½ fl oz) (½ cup) plain yoghurt

With a sharp knife, make a slit all around the centre of the apples to prevent the skins from bursting. Mix together the fig paste, orange rind, orange juice, nuts and butter and fill the apple cavities with the mixture.

Stand the apples in a baking dish, sprinkle with the sugar and pour on the apple juice or water. Bake in the oven at 180 °C, 350 °F, Gas 4, basting occasionally, for 40 minutes, or until the apples are just tender. Stir in the lemon juice and honey 5 minutes before the end of cooking time. Serve with cream and yoghurt beaten together.

Serves 4

Bananas

There is a world of difference between the long, slender strips of peeled, halved and dried bananas, which can be mid-brown and somewhat leathery, and the crisp, crunchy, cream, wafer-thin slivers of freeze-dried banana chips, a disconcertingly 'more-ish' snack. Dried bananas in both of these forms have so many uses – and such a deliciously intensified flavour – that they are worth buying even though the fresh fruit, grown in the tropical regions of Latin America and the West Indies, is a year-round stand-by. To plump up dried banana halves, soak them in warm water for 30 minutes. They are specially good poached with dried apple rings or sliced into apple pie or crumble. For sweet fritters, dry the banana after soaking, dip in a light batter or in egg and cake crumbs and deep-fry until puffed up and golden. For a fast-food dessert, simmer soaked bananas in butter, honey and rum. You can chop the soaked fruit and use it in baking as a change from dates. The teabread recipe below is one example; pastry slices and scones are other possibilities. Freeze-dried banana chips are best enjoyed just as they are – they give a positive 'bite' to cereals and salads and, lightly crushed, make a good instant topping for ice cream and mousses.

Tropical salad

1 small head celery, thinly sliced
125 g (4 oz) (³/₄ cup) whole stoned dates,
*   chopped*
50 g (2 oz) (²/₃ cup) dried banana 'chips'
½ small head Chinese cabbage
*   DRESSING:*
*   60 ml (4 tablespoons) (¼ cup) salad*
*   oil*
*   30 ml (2 tablespoons) cider vinegar*
*   5 ml (1 teaspoon) grated orange rind*
*   salt and freshly ground black pepper*

Mix together the dressing ingredients. Toss the celery, dates and banana chips in the dressing and set aside for 1 hour. Just before serving, line a dish with the Chinese cabbage and spoon on the salad. If you wish, you can toss some thinly sliced Chinese cabbage with the salad shortly before serving.

This salad makes an unusual first course, and is good with cold chicken or ham.

Serves 4–6

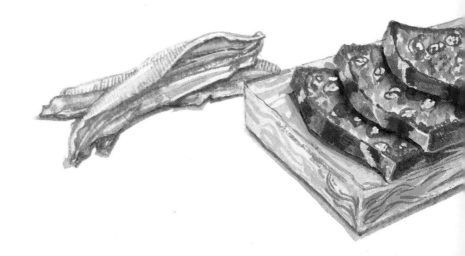

Banana and walnut teabread

175 g (6 oz) dried banana halves
60 ml (4 tablespoons) (¼ cup) orange
  juice
45 ml (3 tablespoons) clear honey
50 g (2 oz) (¼ cup) margarine
275 g (10 oz) (1⅔ cup) wholewheat
  self-raising flour
10 ml (2 teaspoons) baking powder
2.5 ml (½ teaspoon) salt
50 g (2 oz) (¼ cup) molasses sugar
100 g (4 oz) (1 cup) walnuts, chopped
1 egg, beaten
150 ml (¼ pint) (⅔ cup) plain yoghurt
45 ml (3 tablespoons) banana chips,
  crushed

Soak the dried bananas in the orange juice for 30 minutes, drain and chop finely. Melt the honey and margarine and cool slightly. Sift together the flour, baking powder and salt. Stir in the sugar, walnuts, chopped bananas, honey mixture, egg and yoghurt. Beat until smooth. Beat in the banana chips.

Turn the mixture into a greased 500-g (1-lb) loaf-tin and level the top. Bake in the oven at 180 °C, 350 °F, Gas 4 for 1 hour, or until the loaf is well risen and firm. Cool in the tin, then turn out on to a wire rack. When completely cold, store in an airtight tin for 3 days before serving.

Serve sliced. It is very good with cottage cheese.

Makes one 500-g (1-lb) loaf

Candied fruits

Long, golden and sugary strips of candied orange, lemon and citron peel for decorating cakes; boxes of glistening crystallized pineapple rings, apricots, pears and plums for serving as sweetmeats or chopping into creamy desserts; chunks of crystallized ginger for adding spice to apple and rhubarb dishes; and that extra-special luxury, *marrons glacés*, to enjoy with coffee or blend with chestnut and chocolate puddings: these and the many other candied fruits we enjoy, especially at Christmas-time, originated from a practical way of preserving them. The fruits are soaked and then boiled in heavy sugar syrup over a period of several days until they are softened, saturated – and very sticky. That is the candying process, and the fruits can be dried and served or used as they are. They may also be crystallized, that is to say dried and given a hard surface of granulated sugar, or coated with more boiled sugar, which makes them shiny and ice-like – hence the French description, *glacé*. Break off extra-thick layers of hard, sugary coating before using crystallized fruits for baking, and wash and dry glacé cherries. Store dessert fruits between layers of waxed paper; all candied fruits are best kept in airtight containers.

Candied orange peel cake

250 g (8 oz) (²/₃ cup) clear honey
90 ml (6 tablespoons) (¹/₃ cup) vegetable oil
500 g (1 lb) (3 cups) wholewheat flour
salt
5 ml (1 teaspoon) mixed ground spice
5 ml (1 teaspoon) bicarbonate of soda
125 g (4 oz) (¹/₂ cup) light muscovado/ brown sugar
175 g (6 oz) (1 cup) mixed candied orange, lemon and citron peel, finely chopped
3 eggs
45 ml (3 tablespoons) milk
2 large pieces candied orange peel, finely sliced

Heat the honey and oil and cool slightly. Sift together the flour, salt, spices and soda and tip in the bran from the sieve. Stir in the sugar and chopped peel. Add the eggs, the milk and the honey mixture, beating well.

Turn into a greased and lined 21-cm (7-inch) round cake-tin and level the top. Arrange the peel strips in a pattern on top. Bake in the oven at 170 °C, 325 °F, Gas 3 for 1¼ hours or until a skewer pushed into the centre of the cake comes out clean.

Cool on a wire rack, peel off paper and leave until completely cold. Wrap in foil and store in an airtight tin.

Makes one 21-cm (7-inch) cake

Tutti-frutti ice cream

300 ml (¹/₂ pint) (1¹/₄ cups) milk
2 eggs, separated
60 ml (4 tablespoons) (¹/₄ cup) clear honey
30 ml (2 tablespoons) ginger syrup (from jar of preserved ginger)
300 ml (¹/₂ pint) (1¹/₄ cups) plain yoghurt
350 g (6 oz) (1 cup) assorted crystallized fruits, chopped (such as pineapple, papaya, ginger, clementines)

Put the milk and egg yolks in the top of a double boiler or a bowl fitted over a pan of simmering water and stir over low heat. Do not allow the water to boil. When the custard begins to thicken, remove it from the heat and stir in the honey and ginger syrup. Leave to cool. Pour into a chilled container, cover with foil and freeze for 1 hour. Turn the mixture into a chilled bowl and beat until smooth. Whisk the egg whites until stiff and fold them and the yoghurt into the custard. Stir in the chopped fruits. Freeze for 3–4 hours, until the ice cream is firm. Thaw it in the refrigerator for 1 hour before serving. Decorate to taste with sliced candied fruits and 'leaves' of angelica.

Serves 6

NUTS AND SEEDS

The nutritional value of nuts and seeds varies appreciably, but they are all good sources of proteins, carbohydrates, vitamins, fats, minerals and trace elements — the foods stored in concentrated form ready to nurture the next plant generation. As such they are of immense nutritional value to vegetarians, offering in a compact, convenient and deliciously varied form the proteins and fats that would be otherwise lacking in the diet. Nuts range from the small, creamy-white pine kernels that feature prominently in Middle Eastern cuisine to the large, oval and rough-haired coconuts filled with low-calorie 'milk'; seeds come in forms as different as the minute and almost black poppy seeds used to garnish loaves and bread rolls, and the flat, oval, resistantly chewy pumpkin. Increasingly popular combined with dried fruits as snacks, nuts and seeds are incredibly versatile. Use them to make or garnish soup, in salads, sandwiches, bread, pastry and other baking, in meat and fish fillings, casseroles, vegetable dishes and crunchy toppings, in nursery and festive puddings. Buy whole or (cheaper) broken nuts and grind or chop them as you need them: this way you preserve more of the flavour and natural oils. Store in airtight containers in a cool, dry place.

Almonds

As fleshy fruits which enclose a stone and an inner kernel, almonds are actually drupes. First cultivated in Asia Minor, they travelled with the Moslems to Spain and thence to the New World. The State of California is now the world's largest producer of sweet almonds, the harvest beginning in August. The nuts are sold in-shell, shelled and dried, blanched (without the tough, wrinkly brown skin) and sometimes toasted, halved, split, slivered (thinly sliced), nibbed (chopped) and ground, and as almond paste, or marzipan, for cake covering. They contain 20 per cent protein and 600 calories per 100 g (4 oz). For maximum flavour and freshness buy unblanched almonds. Soak for a few minutes in boiling water, drain, then squeeze the nuts out of their skins.

Trout with almonds

4 large rainbow trout, gutted and cleaned
2 lemons
pepper
100 g (4 oz) (½ cup) butter
150 g (5 oz) (1¼ cups) whole, blanched
    almonds
parsley sprigs to garnish

Halve one lemon and squeeze the juice over the fish, both inside and out. Grind pepper over them. Slit the skin diagonally in three places on each side.

Melt half the butter and when hot fry the almonds until browned on all sides. Remove the nuts and heat the remaining butter. Fry the fish over moderate heat for 6 minutes each side or until the fish are just firm.

Serve scattered with the almonds and garnished with lemon wedges and parsley. New potatoes cooked in their skins are a good accompaniment.

Serves 4

Garden salad with almonds

175 g (6 oz) (8 rashers) streaky bacon,
    rinded and cut into squares
1 small cauliflower, cut into florets
125 g (4 oz) (1 cup) blanched, slivered
    almonds

250 g (8 oz) (½ lb) young spinach leaves,
    washed and dried
DRESSING:
150 ml (¼ pint) (⅔ cup) plain
    yoghurt
30 ml (2 tablespoons) cider vinegar
15 ml (1 tablespoon) orange juice
10 ml (2 teaspoons) French mustard
salt and pepper

Fry the bacon squares in a non-stick pan, stirring often, until crisp. Drain, and discard the fat. Steam the cauliflower over boiling water for 3 minutes, plunge it into cold water, drain well and cool. Toast the slivered almonds under a medium grill, turning frequently, for 4–5 minutes, or until golden brown. Cool. Toss together the bacon, cauliflower, almonds and spinach.

Beat together the yoghurt, vinegar, orange juice and mustard and season the dressing to taste with salt and pepper. Pour it over the salad and toss well.

Serves 4

Salted almonds

Use this method for cashews, hazelnuts and peanuts too, and serve with drinks.

250 g (8 oz) (2 cups) blanched whole or
    halved almonds
30 ml (2 teaspoons) vegetable oil
rock salt to taste, about 10 ml (2
    teaspoons)

Pour the oil on a baking tray and spread the nuts in a single layer. Sprinkle on the salt. Roast in the oven at 180 °C, 350 °F, Gas 4 for 8–10 minutes, shaking the tray frequently. Watch that they do not burn. Cool and store in an airtight container.

Makes 250 g (8 oz) (2 cups)

Walnuts

Almost unique among nuts, walnuts contain more polyunsaturated than saturated fat. They are high in vitamins B1, B2 and B5 and rich in phosphorus, magnesium and copper. When fresh, they also contain vitamin C. The highly regarded 'English' walnut, *Juglans regia*, grows throughout Europe and Asia. When the fresh nuts are available in the autumn, moist and almost sweet, they are a delicacy to serve with port and sweet wines. The North American native tree, *Juglans nigra*, the black walnut, has a much stronger flavour. Shelled and halved walnuts with their characteristic scalloped shape are used to decorate both sweet and savoury dishes. Chopped walnuts are used in baking, in salads and make a very good soup with a strong, almost meaty flavour. Pickled walnuts, a traditional accompaniment to cheese and cold meats, game and poultry, do not taste like nuts at all. They are picked in midsummer when the shells are soft and the cases green and preserved in spiced vinegar, when they turn black and shiny. Sliced pickled walnuts are excellent in salads, especially with bland ingredients such as white cabbage and hard-boiled eggs.

Walnut soup

50 g (2 oz) (¼ cup) butter
30 ml (2 tablespoons) wholewheat flour
1.5 litres (2½ pints) (5½ cups) hot
  chicken stock
500 g (1 lb) (4 cups) shelled walnuts,
  ground
salt and pepper
300 ml (½ pint) (1¼ cups) plain
  yoghurt or single/light cream
chopped parsley to garnish

Melt the butter, stir in the flour and when it has formed a paste gradually pour on the stock, stirring. Add the walnuts, season with salt and pepper, cover and simmer gently for 20 minutes. Stir in the yoghurt or cream and heat gently. Taste and adjust the seasoning if needed. If there is a faintly bitter taste (and this can happen if slightly stale walnuts are used) add a little brown sugar or honey. Garnish with the parsley.

Serves 8

Roquefort and walnut mousse

15 g (½ oz) (2 tablespoons) powdered
  gelatine
45 ml (3 tablespoons) orange juice
2 eggs, separated
75 g (3 oz) (¾ cup) chopped walnuts
100 g (4 oz) (¼ lb) Roquefort cheese,
  crumbled
150 ml (¼ pint) (⅔ cup) double/heavy
  cream, beaten
150 ml (¼ pint) (⅔ cup) plain yoghurt
a pinch of cayenne
walnut halves to garnish
black grapes to garnish

Dissolve the gelatine in the orange juice and cool. Beat the egg yolks until stiff. Stir the egg yolks and chopped nuts into the cheese. Stir in the cream, yoghurt and the cooled gelatine. Season with cayenne. Whisk the egg whites until stiff and fold into the mixture. Pour into a wetted square tin and leave in the refrigerator to set for at least 2 hours. Unmould the mousse and garnish the top and sides with halved walnuts and halved and seeded grapes.

Serve the mousse as a starter or a lunch or supper dish with salad.

Serves 6

Brazils

The creamy kernels known as brazil nuts are one of the most highly prized for dessert use and have a rich, almost milky flavour. They grow on tall trees in forests in South America, about twenty nuts closely packed together inside large, woody outer casings the size of coconuts. Brazil nut shells are almost triangular in section and the thin, brown inner skin usually comes away when the nut is cracked. Although brazils are interchangeable with other nuts in salads, soup, rissoles, cakes, pastries, meringue dishes and confectionery, they have a distinctive flavour and always seem to add a touch of luxury.

Hazelnuts

'Nutting', gathering wild hazelnuts from the hedgerows, can be a pleasant and profitable pastime. These small nuts have smooth, shiny round shells. The related and improved filberts and Kentish cobs, with oval shells, are cultivated in Britain, France, Spain, Italy, Turkey and the United States. These nuts are high in vitamin B1, phosphorus, copper and magnesium. They contain over 40 per cent water and are consequently lower than most other nuts in dietary fibre (6.1 per cent) and calories (380 per 100 g/4 oz). Ground hazelnuts, delicious in pastry, cakes and meringues, have a much-improved flavour if they are lightly toasted before further cooking. Spread them on a baking tray and cook them, stirring often, at 180 °C, 350 °F, Gas 4 for about 7–10 minutes.

Brazil-nut toffee

100 g (4 oz) (1 cup) brazils, whole or
  sliced
500 g (1 lb) (2 cups) demerara/brown
  sugar
150 ml (¼ pint) (⅔ cup) water

Grease a 20-cm (8-inch)-square tin and spread the brazils over it. Put the sugar and water into a large, heavy pan and bring to the boil without stirring. Lower the heat once the temperature reaches 126 °C, 260 °F. At this stage, a little of the mixture dropped into cold water will become very brittle – this is called the 'hard crack' stage. Pour the mixture into the tin and spread it evenly. Cool a little, then mark the toffee into squares. When cold, break into pieces and store in an airtight container.

Makes about 500 g (1 lb)

Hazelnut meringue baskets

4 egg whites
250 g (8 oz) (1 cup) light muscovado/
  brown sugar
100 g (4 oz) (1 cup) ground hazelnuts,
  toasted and cooled
5 ml (1 teaspoon) lemon juice
  FILLING:
  50 g (2 oz) (¼ cup) light
    muscovado/brown sugar
  45 ml (3 tablespoons) dark rum
  450-g (15-oz) can unsweetened
    chestnut purée
  25 g (1 oz) (2 tablespoons) butter,
    melted

Whisk the egg whites until stiff. Gradually beat in half the sugar. Mix the remaining sugar with the ground hazelnuts and fold them into the meringue mixture with the lemon juice. Using a piping bag or spoon, spread the mixture on to non-stick silicone paper in 10-cm (4-inch) circles. Spread a 2.5-cm (1-inch)-thick rim around the edge of each circle, making a basket shape. Bake in the oven at 110 °C, 225 °F, Gas ¼ for 1¼ hours, until the meringue is firm and the tops are brown. Cool, then peel off the paper.

For the filling, melt the sugar in the rum. Beat into the chestnut purée, then beat in the melted butter. Cool. Pipe the mixture into the meringue shells up to 1 hour before serving, or push it through a potato 'ricer' to make the traditional 'mont blanc' squiggles.

Serves 6

Note *For a richer filling, beat in 50 g (2 oz) melted chocolate with the butter.*

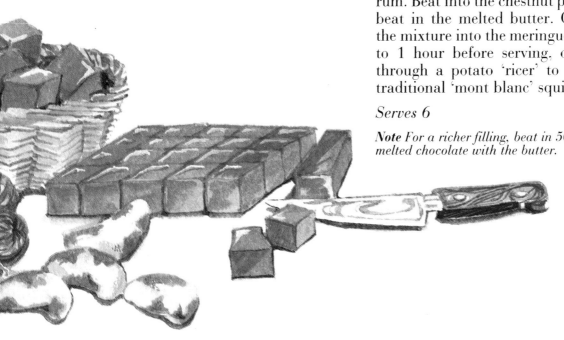

Pecans

With their brightish red, shiny oval shells and long, ridged kernels – which are somewhat similar in appearance to walnuts – pecans, or hickory nuts, are among the most appetizing of all. They are also among the most fattening – as much as three-quarters of their weight consisting of fat. The best-known dish made with this primarily American nut is pecan pie, a classic from the Deep South and the south-west of the USA, where pecan trees flourish. The nuts can be used as an alternative to walnuts and are especially good chopped into vanilla ice cream, coffee or chocolate mousse and into doughnut mixture before baking. Ground pecans make a tasty coating for roast lamb and barbecued chicken, but generally the nuts are used in sweet dishes.

Pine nuts

The seeds of the stone pine, also known as Indian nuts, are small and creamy-white, like enlarged grains of long-grain rice. They are mainly exported by Spain and Italy and are an important source of protein; they may indeed contain over 30 per cent protein. Pine nuts, which are always sold ready shelled, have a softer texture than most dessert nuts and are very good raw, scattered on to fresh fruit salads, compote of dried fruits, and mixed in green salads of all kinds. In Italian cooking they are mixed with mushrooms, spinach or other vegetables as a filling for rolled meat 'parcels'. In the Middle East they are used extensively – with fruit, in milk puddings, pilaffs and with poultry. They are also available roasted and salted and, as a sweetmeat, covered in chocolate. Pine nuts are very expensive. Blanched and slivered almonds, though stronger in flavour, may be substituted.

Pecan pie

250 g (8 oz) (1½ cups) wholewheat flour
a pinch of salt
50 g (2 oz) (¼ cup) white vegetable fat
65 g (2½ oz) (⅓ cup) margarine
25 g (1 oz) (¼ cup) ground pecans
5 ml (1 teaspoon) lemon juice
  FILLING:
  4 eggs
  350 g (12 oz) (1 cup) golden or corn
    syrup
  25 g (1 oz) (2 tablespoons) butter,
    melted
  5 ml (1 teaspoon) vanilla essence
  150 g (5 oz) (1¼ cups) pecans
  1 egg yolk, beaten

Sift the flour and salt, tip in the bran from the sieve and rub in the fats. Stir in the ground pecans and lemon juice and mix with just enough water to make a firm dough. Cover and chill for 30 minutes. Roll out the dough on a lightly floured board, use to line a 20-cm (8-inch)-square tin and trim the edges. Set aside for 30 minutes.

Beat the eggs and syrup and beat in the melted butter and vanilla. Chop half the pecans and stir them into the mixture. Pour into the pastry case and brush the pastry with egg yolk. Bake in the oven at 200 °C, 400 °F, Gas 6 for 30 minutes. Reduce oven temperature to 160 °C, 325 °F, Gas 3. Arrange the reserved nuts on top of the pie and continue baking for 25–30 minutes, or until the filling is set. Serve warm or cold, with yoghurt.

Serves 6–8

Turkey and pine nut rolls

4 slices of turkey breast, about 100 g
  (4 oz) each
75 g (3 oz) (⅓ cup) butter
1 small onion, finely chopped
100 g (4 oz) (¼ lb) mushrooms, chopped
60 ml (4 tablespoons) (¼ cup)
  wholewheat breadcrumbs
30 ml (2 tablespoons) chopped parsley
60 ml (4 tablespoons) (¼ cup) pine nuts
salt and pepper
  SAUCE:
  15 ml (1 tablespoon) wholewheat flour
  150 ml (¼ pint) (⅔ cup) hot chicken
    stock
  2 oranges
  60 ml (4 tablespoons) (¼ cup) double/
    heavy cream

Beat the turkey slices with a rolling-pin to flatten them. Melt half the butter and fry the onion for 2 minutes over moderate heat. Add the mushrooms for 2 minutes. Then remove from the heat and stir in the breadcrumbs, parsley and nuts. Season with salt and pepper and leave to cool.

Divide the filling between the turkey slices and roll up, swiss-roll/jelly roll style. Tie with fine twine. Fry the turkey rolls in the remaining butter for 6–7 minutes, turning them frequently to brown on all sides. Remove from the pan and keep warm.

Stir the flour into the pan, pour on the stock and stir until it is smooth. Squeeze the juice of both oranges and add to the sauce with the grated rind of 1 orange. Bring to the boil, season with salt and pepper and simmer for 3 minutes. Return the turkey rolls to the pan and simmer for 5 minutes. Stir in the cream, remove the strings and serve.

Glazed carrots and broccoli scattered with pine nuts and chopped bacon are good accompaniments.

Serves 4

Cashews

Native to Brazil, cashews are grown commercially in tropical regions of India, Egypt, East Africa and the West Indies. The trees produce edible fleshy fruits, at the base of which hang the nuts. A toxic oil between the shell and the kernel has to be driven off by roasting before the shells can be cracked. Inside are the sweet-tasting, pale cream and slightly kidney-shaped nuts which are sold whole, halved or in broken pieces. The nuts should be firm and slightly crumbly: softness indicates staleness. Cashews are specially good in curries, pilaffs, stir-fried with vegetables or meat and as a garnish. Roasted and salted cashews, which are easy to prepare at home (see page 27), are sold as a cocktail snack.

Chestnuts

Sweet chestnuts roasting in their shells over an open fire have one of the most irresistible of smells. There's often plenty of resistance, though, to shelling the nuts for cooking – it can be tedious. Slit the shells and shake the nuts in a pan with a little oil over moderate heat, or grill them. When the skins blacken and crack, peel off the shell and tough brown inner skins together. Alternatively, boil the nuts for 10–15 minutes before shelling. Shelled chestnuts may be cooked by steaming or boiling in milk, water or stock. They can be served as a vegetable or tossed with, for example, brussels sprouts or cauliflower, which take well to their sweetness. Grind the nuts to make purée for puddings and chestnut stuffing, which is traditional with festive poultry. Chestnuts are sold dried and shelled, to be reconstituted in water, and canned or bottled (also shelled). Chestnut purée is sold both sweetened and 'au naturel'. Peeled chestnuts boiled several times in heavy syrup become the sweetmeat *marrons glacés*.

Cashew-nut griddle scones

250 g (8 oz) (1½ cups) wholewheat
    self-raising flour
10 ml (2 teaspoons) baking powder
2.5 ml (½ teaspoon) salt
50 g (2 oz) (¼ cup) margarine
75 g (3 oz) (¾ cup) ground, toasted
    cashews
45 ml (3 tablespoons) demerara/brown
    sugar
grated rind and juice of ½ orange
150 ml (¼ pint) (⅔ cup) milk

Sift the flour, baking powder and salt and
tip in any bran from the sieve. Rub in the
margarine until the mixture is like fine
breadcrumbs. Stir in the ground cashews,
sugar, orange rind and juice and the milk
and mix to a soft dough. Roll out on a lightly
floured board and cut into rounds with a
5-cm (2-inch) cutter.

Heat a griddle or heavy frying-pan until it
is very hot. Grease it lightly and cook the
scones for 7–8 minutes on each side. Serve
with cashew butter, made as for peanut
butter (page 37).

Makes about 12 scones

Aubergines/eggplants with chestnut filling

4 small aubergines/eggplants, halved
salt
45 ml (3 tablespoons) vegetable oil
1 small onion, finely chopped
1 clove garlic, finely chopped
1 green pepper, seeded and finely chopped
2 large tomatoes, skinned
5 ml (1 teaspoon) mixed dried herbs
a pinch of grated nutmeg
250 g (8 oz) canned unsweetened chestnut
    purée
pepper
60 ml (4 tablespoons) (¼ cup) sultanas

Scoop the flesh from the aubergines/
eggplants without breaking the skins. Put
the flesh in a colander, sprinkle with salt
and set aside for 45 minutes to drain off the
bitter juices. Rinse and dry thoroughly, then
chop. Melt the oil and fry the onion, garlic
and pepper for 3–4 minutes over moderate
heat. Chop and add the tomatoes with the
herbs and nutmeg and stir to mix well. In a
bowl, beat the chestnut purée and beat in
the vegetables. Season with salt and pepper
and stir in the sultanas.

Pile the filling into the aubergine/
eggplant shells and place in a single layer in
a greased baking dish. Cover the dish and
bake in the oven at 180 °C, 350 °F, Gas 4 for
25–30 minutes. Serve with tomato sauce.

Serves 4

Roast and salted chestnuts

Prick the shells of the chestnuts and spread
them on a baking sheet. Roast them in the
oven at 220 °C, 425 °F, Gas 7 for 15–20
minutes. Peel off the shells and inner skins
while still hot and toss in salt. Serve hot. Or
cook the nuts in a slotted shovel or on a wire
rack over a barbecue or open fire. Always
prick the shells first, or the nuts will
explode.

*500 g (1 lb) chestnuts yield about 325 g
    (11 oz) shelled nuts*

Peanuts

Because of their unusual underground growing habit, peanuts are also known as groundnuts and earth nuts. They are in fact the pods of a leguminous plant which penetrate the soil from above and mature into beige, brittle, crinkly shells containing up to four nuts or seeds. They come from India, East and West Africa, the Far East and the southern states of the USA. The nuts are hard and smooth with brown or pink skins which rub off easily. They are sold roasted in the shell; shelled and roasted with oil and salt; dry-roasted, sometimes with a 'barbecue' flavouring, or shelled and unroasted. To roast peanuts, spread them on a baking tray and cook in the oven, at 200° C, 400° F, Gas 6 for about 10 minutes, shaking the tray frequently. Rub off the skins in a tea-towel. Peanuts can contain up to 28 per cent protein, and are an important part of vegetarian régimes. Use them in salads with chopped cabbage, celery and apple, in bread, biscuits/cookies and cakes, and in confectionery such as peanut toffee. You can buy the nuts coated with chocolate, as a snack. Peanut butter, in both its smooth and its crunchy form, is a popular spread with children and simple to make (see recipe).

Peanut bread

200 g (7 oz) (1¼ cups) wholewheat flour
5 ml (1 teaspoon) baking powder
5 ml (1 teaspoon) bicarbonate of soda
50 g (2 oz) (¼ cup) margarine
75 g (3 oz) (⅓ cup) light muscovado/
  brown sugar
75 g (3 oz) (¾ cup) salted peanuts,
  roughly chopped
25 g (1 oz) (2 tablespoons) peanut butter
about 120 ml (8 tablespoons) (½ cup)
  milk

Line the base and sides of a used 900-ml (1½-pint) (30 fl oz) food can with non-stick silicone paper. Sift together the flour, baking powder and soda, tip in the bran from the sieve and rub in the margarine until the mixture is like fine crumbs. Stir in the sugar and peanuts then mix in the peanut butter and enough milk to make a soft dough. Spoon into the can, stand it upright on a baking sheet and cover the top with a greased baking sheet.

Bake in the oven at 180°C, 350°F, Gas 4 for 1 hour or until the loaf is cooked. A skewer inserted into the middle should come out clean. Cool on a wire rack. When cold, turn out of the tin, wrap in foil and store in an airtight tin for at least 2 days before eating. Serve spread with butter or thick fruit purée such as apricot or apple.

Makes one 500-g (1-lb) loaf

Peanut butter cookies

75 g (3 oz) (⅓ cup) margarine
175 g (6 oz) (¾ cup) light muscovado/
  brown sugar
1 egg
100 g (4 oz) (½ cup) peanut butter
175 g (6 oz) (1 cup) wholewheat flour
5 ml (1 teaspoon) bicarbonate of soda
a pinch of salt
15 ml (1 tablespoon) milk
currants for features

Beat the margarine and sugar until light and fluffy, then beat in the egg and peanut butter. Sift the flour, soda and salt and gradually add to the butter mixture. Stir in the bran from the sieve and the milk and mix to form a dough.

Roll out on a lightly floured board and cut into shapes – children love using the gingerbread-man cutter! Place on an ungreased baking sheet and flatten the tops with a fork. Bake in the top of the oven at 220°C, 425°F, Gas 7 for 10–12 minutes, until golden brown. Press in currants for facial features and 'buttons' immediately, before the cookies harden. Cool on a wire rack.

Makes about 12, according to size

Peanut butter

250 g (8 oz) (2 cups) roasted unsalted
  peanuts
30 ml (2 tablespoons) vegetable oil
2.5 ml (½ teaspoon) lemon juice
salt to taste

Drop the peanuts a few at a time on to the rotating blades of an electric blender or food processor. Add the oil and lemon juice and process to a paste. Add salt if wished. Store in the refrigerator in an airtight container.

Makes about 250 g (8 oz) (2 cups)

Coconut

The tropical islands of the Indian Ocean, Sri Lanka and New Guinea are the main producers of coconuts. The huge egg-shaped nuts, covered in thick fibres and a tough brown skin, have a layer about 2.5 cm (1 inch) thick of creamy-white moist flesh. The hollow centres contain a sweet juice known as coconut milk. To open a coconut, pierce the flesh with a skewer in two places and drain off the milk – it makes a delicious drink and is also good in sweet sauces and curries. Bake the nut in a medium-hot oven for 15 minutes, then crack it open with a hammer. Peel off the brown skin and grate the flesh. Fresh coconuts are not readily obtainable and the flesh is more familiar in its grated or shredded and dried form, desiccated coconut. This is used in cakes, biscuits/cookies and sweet puddings, as well as to flavour meringues and garnish curries. You can also buy blocks of compressed coconut, coconut 'cream', which look like vegetable fat. This is used in cakes and confectionery, particularly with chocolate.

Pistachios

Pistachios come from India, the Mediterranean and the southern states of the USA. They are oval, about 1 cm (⅓ inch) long, bright green with a red-tinged skin (which is edible) and very tough shells which, luckily, split as the nuts ripen. They are sold in the shell, shelled, and salted, for cocktail savouries. They make excellent additions to smooth-textured pâtés and terrines, to pilaff, ice cream and confections.

Mint and pistachio ice cream

75 g (3 oz) (⅓ cup) light muscovado/
    brown sugar
150 ml (¼ pint) (⅔ cup) water
50 g (2 oz) (5 cups) young mint leaves
juice of 1 lemon
150 ml (¼ pint) (⅔ cup) plain yoghurt
150 ml (¼ pint) (⅔ cup) double/heavy
    cream, whipped
40 g (1½ oz) (⅓ cup) pistachios,
    chopped
sprigs of mint to garnish

Bring the sugar and water to the boil, add the mint leaves and set aside to cool. Strain the syrup and stir in the lemon juice, yoghurt and cream and mix thoroughly. Stir in the pistachios. Spoon into an empty ice-cube tray, cover with foil and freeze for 45 minutes. Tip into a chilled bowl and beat to break down the ice crystals. Return to the container, cover and freeze for 2 hours.

Transfer to the refrigerator to mellow for 30 minutes before serving. Decorate with mint sprigs.

Serves 4–6

Note *Wholewheat shortbread or muesli biscuits/cookies make good accompaniments. Small scoops of the ice cream are a delightful addition to chilled fresh fruit.*

Halva with pistachios

125 g (4 oz) (¹/2 cup) butter
750 g (1¹/2 lb) (3 cups) light muscovado/
  brown sugar
3 eggs
200 ml (7 fl oz) (⁷/8 cup) milk
75 g (3 oz) (¹/2 cup) wholewheat flour
10 ml (2 teaspoons) baking powder
salt
375 g (12 oz) (1²/3 cup) wholewheat
  semolina
125 g (4 oz) (1 cup) pistachios, halved
600 ml (1 pint) (2¹/2 cups) water
grated rind and juice of 1 lemon
1 stick cinnamon
45 ml (3 tablespoons) clear honey

Cream together the butter and 250 g (8 oz) (1 cup) of the sugar until light and fluffy. Beat the eggs and milk and mix together the flour, baking powder, salt and semolina. Gradually add the milk and the semolina mixtures alternately to the creamed butter. Stir in the nuts. Spread the halva mixture into a greased baking tin 23 × 18 cm (9 × 7 inches). Bake in the oven at 180° C, 350° F, Gas 4 for 45 minutes.

Bring to the boil the water, remaining sugar, lemon rind and juice, cinnamon and honey and simmer for 5 minutes. Remove the cinnamon and pour over the halva as soon as it is cooked. Leave to cool. Cut into squares and wrap in foil. Store in the refrigerator.

Makes about 1 kg (2¹/4 lb)

Coconut meringue pie

wholewheat shortcrust pastry, made with
  250 g (8 oz) (1¹/3 cups) flour (page 57)
45 ml (3 tablespoons) cornflour/cornstarch
700 ml (1¹/4 pints) (3 cups) milk
125 g (4 oz) (¹/2 cup) light muscovado/
  brown sugar
4 eggs, separated
250 g (8 oz) (2¹/2 cups) desiccated coconut
45 ml (3 tablespoons) demerara/brown
  sugar

Roll out the pastry and line a 25-cm (10-inch) greased flan ring on a baking sheet. Prick the base, line with greased foil, fill with baking beans and bake in the oven at 200° C, 400° F, Gas 6 for 10 minutes. Remove the foil and beans and continue baking for 5 minutes.

Mix the cornflour/cornstarch to a smooth paste with a little of the milk. Bring the remaining milk to the boil and pour on to the cornflour/cornstarch mixture, stirring constantly. Return to the pan, bring to the boil and simmer for 3 minutes, stirring. Remove from the heat and stir in the muscovado/brown sugar, egg yolks and all but 50 g (2 oz) (¹/2 cup) of the coconut. Pour into the flan case and bake for 15 minutes.

Whisk the egg whites until stiff, then fold in the demerara/brown sugar and remaining coconut. Spread over the coconut pie. Lower the oven heat to 140° C, 275° F, Gas 1 and bake for 15–20 minutes.

Serves 6

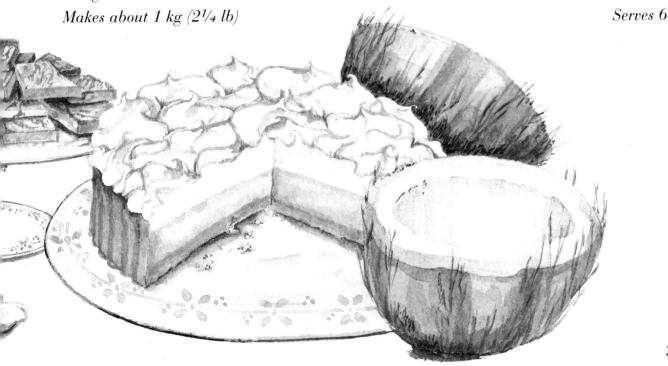

Sprouting seeds and beans

Many types of seeds and beans can be 'planted' in a jar to produce an indoor garden of crisp, crunchy, vitamin-packed sprouts. Try sprouting alfalfa, spicy fenugreek and sunflower seeds (non-roasted, whole lentils, aduki, soya and mung beans – which produce Chinese bean sprouts – and chick peas. Depending on size, they will sprout within 2–6 days and can yield up to ten times their original weight.

Put about 45 ml (3 tablespoons) seeds in a jar and tie a piece of cheesecloth or muslin over the top. Fill the jar with tepid water, shake well and drain. Place the jar on its side in a drawer and each day fill it again with tepid water, shake and drain. The sprouts are ready when they are about 5 cm (2 inches) long. Wash them, drain well and use as soon as possible. To store, put in cold water in a

covered container in the refrigerator and change the water after 24 hours. Store for a maximum of two days. Some seeds such as soya and mung beans and chick peas respond better if first soaked in water overnight.

Serve the sprouts as a salad, as a filling for vegetable pies and samosas, in soups and casseroles, or briefly stir-fried.

Other seeds

Like nuts, plant seeds are a good source of phosphorus, which combines with the B vitamins; potassium, which helps to regulate both blood pressure and the water balance in the body and stimulates the growth of soft tissue; and iron, which is needed to build the red haemoglobin and carry oxygen through the body. Added to that, they are very high in dietary fibre, the natural roughage. With such credentials, seeds are well worth considering in all kinds of culinary ways, in muesli, snacks and salads, as a garnish for soups, meat and fish dishes, casseroles, vegetables and puddings, or as a crunchy topping for bread, biscuits/cookies and cakes.

Many seeds, mainly those gathered from aromatic plants grown in the tropics, are highly pungent, and are used as spices. See pages 101–2. Others have a mild flavour: some, like pumpkin seeds, almost sweet, and others, like sesame, more nutty. Melon, poppy and sunflower seeds are also worth trying.

Nut and seed loaf

125 g (4 oz) (³/₄ cup) raw sunflower
  seeds
50 g (2 oz) (¹/₃ cup) sesame seeds
60 ml (4 tablespoons) (¹/₄ cup) vegetable
  oil
2 large onions, finely chopped
2 cloves garlic, finely chopped
1 green pepper, seeded and finely chopped
50 g (2 oz) (¹/₂ cup) hazelnuts, ground
50 g (2 oz) (¹/₂ cup) blanched almonds,
  ground
125 g (4 oz) (1¹/₃ cups) wholewheat
  breadcrumbs
150 ml (¹/₄ pint) (²/₃ cup) vegetable
  stock
45 ml (3 tablespoons) tamari sauce
60 ml (4 tablespoons) (¹/₄ cup) chopped
  herbs
salt and pepper

Toast the seeds in a frying-pan over moderate heat for 3–4 minutes, stirring frequently. Cool. Heat the oil and fry the onion, garlic and green pepper for 3–4 minutes. Mix together the seeds, vegetables, nuts, breadcrumbs, stock, sauce and herbs. Season to taste. Turn into a greased 900-g (2-lb) tin and bake at 180° C, 350° F, Gas 4 for 50 minutes. Serve hot, with tomato sauce and green salad.

Serves 6

PULSES

Broad beans (fava beans in the US) are the only pulses native to Europe. The whole family of kidney beans in all its forms and colours – red, white, pink, green, yellow, purple, brown, black, flecked, speckled and spotted – originated in the Americas and was one of the rich rewards when the New World was discovered in the sixteenth century. These pulses, though they differ so markedly in appearance, are largely interchangeable in cooking. Just adjust cooking times accordingly.

Soya beans, richest of all in protein, are native to Asia and have been one of the staple foods of that continent for thousands of years. Alone among pulses, soya beans contain all the amino acids the body needs and rank with eggs, meat, fish and dairy produce as first-class proteins. Other pulses must be eaten with a grain or dairy product at the same meal to complete the nutritional needs – hence the great British snack of beans on toast, the black beans and rice of African soul food, and lima beans with corn, the American succotash.

Dried pulses have been of enormous nutritional significance across the world since ancient times. Now, when the threat of a world protein shortage looms and the value of dietary fibre is widely appreciated, they still have a vitally important part to play. Beans and peas have been taken to the hearts of all cultures and creeds, cooked in all manner of ways in all extremes of climate. The following recipes give some idea of their versatility.

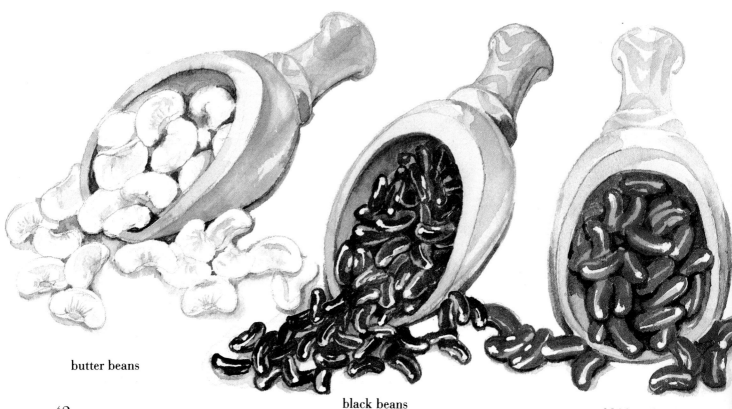

butter beans

black beans

red kidney beans

Soaking and cooking dried pulses

All dried pulses, except orange or red lentils, need soaking to begin the rehydration process before cooking. Wash the pulses first and discard any discoloured ones and those that float to the top of the water.

Pulses absorb about two-and-a-half times their volume during soaking, so put them in a roomy container with plenty of water. The 'slow method' is to soak them in cold water for several hours. The 'quick method' is to put them in a large pan of cold water, bring them to the boil and boil for 2 minutes. When the water has cooled they are ready to cook. Drain the pulses and discard the soaking water.

A word of warning: all kidney beans must be cooked in fast-boiling water for at least 12 minutes to kill harmful toxins. *Never* add them to simmering casseroles without first taking this essential precaution.

Cooking times vary according to the variety and age of the pulses. One golden rule is *never* to add salt until just before the cooking time is up. Salt them at the beginning and pulses will *never* soften!

Cook pulses in water, unsalted vegetable or meat stock, with added herbs, spices, vegetables or citrus rinds for flavouring.

Lentils, mung beans and split peas have the shortest cooking time, up to *1 hour*.

Aduki beans, butter (calico) beans, flageolets, white haricot beans and red kidney beans may take *1–1½ hours*.

Black-eyed beans, borlotti beans, broad (fava) beans and pinto beans may need *2–2½ hours*.

Black (turtle) beans, gungo peas and whole dried peas may need *2–3 hours*.

And longest of all, chick peas and soya beans might take *3–3½ hours*.

All these cooking times may be cut considerably by using a pressure cooker: for example, lentils take 10 minutes and chick peas 45 minutes, both at high pressure.

Long, slow cooking in the oven or an electric crock-pot is ideal once beans and peas have been partly cooked by boiling. Without this they will remain obstinately tough. Allow 30–60 minutes pre-cooking, according to type, and up to 8 hours' slow cooking.

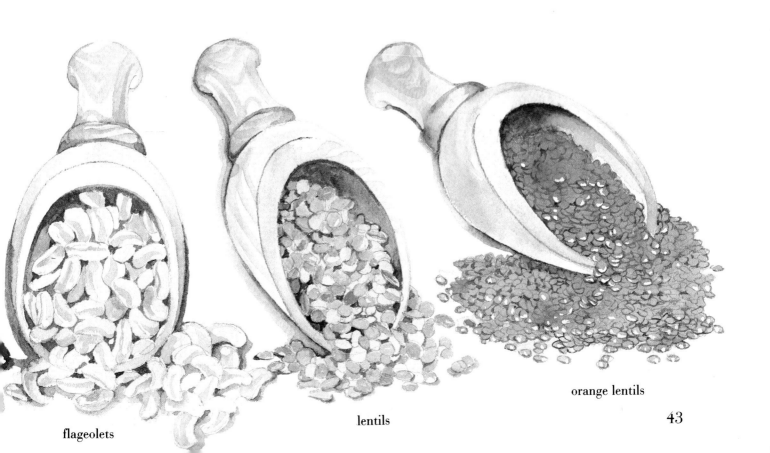

flageolets

lentils

orange lentils

First courses

Apart from hearty country soups and chilled, refreshing salads – which follow – there are all manner of ways of presenting pulses appetizingly to start a meal. The creamy, glossy chick-pea paste, *hummus*, is a familiar favourite on Greek and Middle Eastern menus. You can serve it as a dip with pitta, crackers or fresh vegetable crudités as dip-sticks, as a sandwich filling or part of a salad course. For tasty snacks, spoon the paste into slices of celery or seeded cucumber chunks. Experiment with other pulses, too. Cook red lentils to a (much quicker) purée and beat them to a paste with softened butter, tomato purée and lemon juice, or flavour puréed Indian brown lentils with curry paste and chopped onion. Purée cooked haricot beans with butter, garlic and fresh herbs, and beat flageolet purée with mashed avocado, herbs and orange juice. All these purées make more substantial 'openers' if packed into hollowed-out raw tomatoes or lightly cooked vegetables – courgettes/zucchini, aubergines/eggplant or peppers – and served either chilled or piping hot, topped with cheese and grilled. You can fill vegetables with bean salads, too, for a feast of flavour and texture contrast. Serving the foods in such ways makes a little go further.

Hummus (chick-pea paste)

250 g (8 oz) (1⅓ cups) cooked chick peas
125 g (4 oz) (⅓ cup) tahina (sesame-seed paste)
2 cloves garlic
120 ml (8 tablespoons) (½ cup) olive oil, plus extra to garnish
sea salt and pepper
30 ml (2 tablespoons) chopped parsley (broad-leaved type if available) to garnish

Set aside 50 g (2 oz) (⅓ cup) of the cooked peas. Purée the remainder in an electric blender or food processor with the *tahina*, lemon juice, garlic and olive oil. Or put the peas through a mouli-legumes and beat them together with the other ingredients. Season to taste with salt and pepper.

Pile the *hummus* into a dish, garnish with the chick peas and parsley and dribble a little olive oil to glisten. Serve as a dip with hot pitta bread, crackers or crudités and wholewheat rolls, or as suggested above.

Serves 6–8

Pitta

500 g (1 lb) (3 cups) wholewheat flour
10 ml (2 teaspoons) salt
1 sachet (¼ oz) dried fast-action yeast
5 ml (1 teaspoon) clear honey
300 ml (½ pint) (1¼ cups) warm water

Sift together the flour and salt, tip in the bran and stir in the yeast. Dissolve the honey in the water and add to the dry ingredients. Mix to a dough. Knead on a lightly floured board until smooth. Cover with a damp cloth and leave in a warm place for 1 hour to rise.

Knead again and divide into 6 pieces. Roll each one to an oval about 20 × 12 cm (8 × 5 inches), place on a floured board, cover and leave to rise for 20 minutes.

Heat 2 baking sheets in the oven at 230°C, 450°F, Gas 8. Place the pittas on them and bake for 15 minutes until the pittas are brown at the edges. Serve warm.

Makes 6

Bean-bag courgettes/zucchini

4 medium courgettes/zucchini
salt
4 canned artichoke hearts, drained and
*   sliced*
125 g (4 oz) (½ cup) cooked red kidney
*   beans*
3 spring/green onions, trimmed and finely
*   chopped*
30 ml (2 tablespoons) fresh summer
*   savory, or chopped parsley*
2 hard-boiled eggs, quartered, to garnish
DRESSING:
*   1 clove garlic, crushed*
*   grated rind and juice of ½ orange*
*   45 ml (3 tablespoons) olive oil*
*   15 ml (1 tablespoon) cider vinegar*
*   30 ml (2 tablespoons) plain yoghurt*
*   salt and pepper*

Trim the courgettes/zucchini, split them in half lengthways and steam them for 5 minutes over boiling, salted water. Pat them dry and leave to cool.

Mix together the artichoke hearts, cooked beans, chopped onion and herbs. Mix together the garlic, orange rind and juice, oil, vinegar and yoghurt and season the dressing with salt and pepper. Pour on to the bean mixture and toss well. Pile the salad into the courgettes/zucchini and garnish with egg wedges. Serve chilled.

Serves 4

Soups

Dried pulses have an important contribution to make to soups of all kinds and all nationalities, whether they form one of the main ingredients, puréed into thick, smooth soups or whole in meat or vegetable chowders, or are added on the point of serving to give extra protein, dietary fibre, colour and texture. Split-pea soup made with bacon stock is a trusty old country favourite (see recipe) which has its counterpart in Indian cooking, in which dal soup is spiced with ground ginger, turmeric and cayenne. Try cooking butter beans with diced salt pork and potatoes for a version of New England chowder, and add red or black beans to oxtail and other meat soups. A handful of cooked pulses stored in the refrigerator makes a nutritious last-minute addition to all manner of soups. Try flageolets with leek soup, and pinto beans to complement the grated beetroot of borscht.

Garnishes are important too. A spoonful of chopped herbs or a sprinkling of spice adds welcome colour, but that's not an end to the matter. Remember that garnishes give you the chance to fill the nutritional gaps left by all pulses except soya. Add wholewheat pasta shapes to beany broths, croûtons of wholemeal bread tossed in sesame seed (grains) to smooth, creamy bean soups; stir raw beaten eggs into piping hot clear soups (bean minestrone, for example) to cook in the broth, swirl yoghurt or cream over spicy mixtures, and add cubes of cheese (all dairy products) to chowders.

Minestrone soup

60 ml (4 tablespoons) (¼ cup) olive oil
1 medium onion, thinly sliced
3 medium carrots, thinly sliced
2 medium potatoes, peeled and diced
2 cloves garlic, finely chopped
5 ml (1 teaspoon) dried oregano
5 ml (1 teaspoon) dried thyme
1.25 litres (2¼ pints) (5½ cups)
*   vegetable or chicken stock*
2 small courgettes/zucchini, sliced
375 g (12 oz) (¾ lb) tomatoes, skinned
*   and sliced*
125 g (4 oz) (½ cup) cooked dried
*   haricot beans*
50 g (2 oz) (½ cup) wholewheat
*   short-cut macaroni*
salt and pepper
grated Parmesan cheese to serve

Heat the oil and fry the onion, carrots, potatoes and garlic over moderate heat for 3–4 minutes, stirring once or twice. Add the herbs and stock, bring to the boil, cover and simmer for 15 minutes. Add the courgettes/zucchini, tomatoes and beans and simmer for a further 15 minutes. Add the macaroni, season with salt and pepper, return to the boil, cover and cook for 12–15 minutes more, until the pasta is just tender. Serve the cheese separately.

Serves 6–8

Split-pea soup

25 g (1 oz) (2 tablespoons) margarine
1 large onion, sliced
1 medium potato, peeled and diced
2 medium carrots, sliced
5 ml (1 teaspoon) ground turmeric
175 g (6 oz) (¾ cup) dried yellow split
   peas, soaked and drained
1 knuckle of bacon
1.25 litres (2¼ pints) (5½ cups) water
1 bouquet garni
2 bay leaves
salt and pepper
45 ml (3 tablespoons) single/light cream
   CROÛTONS:
   2 2-cm (¾-inch) thick slices wholemeal
      bread, cut into cubes
   40 g (1½ oz) (3 tablespoons)
      margarine
   45 ml (3 tablespoons) chopped parsley

Melt the margarine and fry the onion, potato and carrots over moderate heat for 3–4 minutes, stirring once or twice. Stir in the turmeric. Add the split peas, knuckle of bacon, water, bouquet garni and bay leaves and bring to the boil. Skim any scum from the surface, cover the pan and simmer for 1½ hours. Remove the bacon and bay leaves. Liquidize the stock and vegetables in a blender or food processor, or put through a mouli-legumes or sieve. Return to the pan. Cut the skin from the bacon. Cut off the meat, chop it into cubes and stir into the soup. Re-heat gently, season and stir in the cream.

   To make the croûtons, fry the bread cubes in the margarine, stirring often, until they are dry and crisp. Toss them at once in the parsley. Serve them separately.

Serves 6

Note *Pulses of all kinds can be used to make soup in this way. Red kidney-bean soup is usually spiced and black bean soup garnished with rice. The colour of these puréed soups, incidentally, is less attractive than the flavour.*

Haricot bean chowder

25 g (1 oz) (2 tablespoons) margarine
1 large onion, sliced
6 rashers streaky bacon, rinded and cut
   into squares
125 g (4 oz) (⅔ cup) dried haricot beans,
   soaked and drained
1.25 litres (2¼ pints) (5½ cups)
   chicken stock
375 g (12 oz) (¾ lb) potatoes, peeled
   and diced
300 ml (½ pint) (1¼ cups) milk
125-g (4-oz) can (⅔ cup) sweetcorn,
   drained
salt and pepper
75 g (3 oz) (¾ cup) cheese, cubed
15 ml (1 tablespoon) chopped parsley to
   garnish

Melt the margarine and fry the onion and bacon over moderate heat for 4–5 minutes, stirring once or twice. Add the beans and stock, bring to the boil and fast-boil for 12 minutes. Cover, lower the heat and simmer for 1 hour. Add the potatoes, milk and sweetcorn and simmer for 20 minutes. Season with salt and pepper. Stir in the cheese just before serving. Garnish with the parsley.

Serves 6–8

Salads

Think of salads and you think of lettuce and tomato? Lettuce contains 1.5 per cent dietary fibre and 1.0 per cent protein, and tomatoes slightly less. Think in terms of pulses for salads and the count goes up considerably. Cooked pulses have about 5.0 per cent fibre and 7.0 per cent protein – and can be absolutely delicious. When you are cooking beans, peas and lentils for other dishes, it makes sense – because of long cooking times – to over-cater and store some in lidded containers in the refrigerator. Toss kidney beans – red, black or white – with chopped apple, raw leek and sunflower seeds in an orange vinaigrette dressing; add pale green flageolets to a salad of chopped red cabbage and raisins. Serve a salad of whole lentils, glistening with red wine dressing, on a bed of endive and watercress and garnished with egg wedges – and go on and on inventing ways of your own.

Pulses for salads should be well cooked but not mushy and are best served chilled. Ring the changes by replacing the vinegar in a French dressing with orange, lemon, grapefruit, apple or pineapple juice, red or white wine or sherry. A little plain yoghurt beaten in with the acid ingredient and oil makes a pleasant change too. And for a fibre-full dressing, thin down any left-over *hummus* or other bean paste with oil and lemon juice – it is surprisingly good.

Three-bean salad

125 g (4 oz) (1/2 cup) cooked dried red
  kidney beans
125 g (4 oz) (1/2 cup) cooked dried chick
  peas
250 g (8 oz) (1/2 lb) fresh bean shoots
4 spring/green onions, trimmed and sliced
1 small onion, thinly sliced into rings
45 ml (3 tablespoons) chopped parsley
  (broad-leaved if available)
young spinach or lettuce leaves to serve
  DRESSING:
  75 ml (5 tablespoons) (1/3 cup) salad
    oil
  grated rind and juice of 1/2 orange
  15 ml (1 tablespoon) cider vinegar
  salt and pepper

Mix the dressing ingredients together and toss in the kidney beans and chick peas. Leave for about 30 minutes. Toss in the bean shoots, onions and herbs. Arrange the salad on a plate of spinach or lettuce leaves. Serve chilled.

Serves 6

Note *Many other combinations make good pulse salads, and especially 'three-bean' salads. Use any dried beans or peas in place of those suggested. Butter beans, pinto beans and mung beans, for example, complement each other well.*

Salade niçoise

250 g (8 oz) (1/2 lb) young whole french
  beans, topped and tailed
salt
50 g (2 oz) (1/4 cup) cooked dried
  flageolets
50 g (2 oz) (1/4 cup) cooked dried haricot
  beans
1 green pepper, seeded and sliced
1/2 small cucumber, diced
4 spring/green onions, thinly sliced
4 firm tomatoes, skinned and quartered
lettuce leaves to serve
175-g (6-oz) can tuna fish, flaked and
  drained
50-g (2-oz) can anchovy fillets, drained
  and halved
12 black olives
  DRESSING:
  60 ml (4 tablespoons) (1/4 cup) salad
    oil
  5 ml (1 teaspoon) lemon juice
  15 ml (1 tablespoon) white wine
    vinegar
  2.5 ml (1/2 teaspoon) mustard powder
  1 clove garlic, crushed
  pepper

Mix together the dressing ingredients.

Cook the french beans in salted water until barely tender. Drain, plunge into cold water to cool and drain again. Toss together the dried beans, green pepper, cucumber, spring/green onions, half the tomatoes, tuna fish and anchovies. Pour on the dressing and toss well.

Line a bowl with lettuce leaves, pile on the salad and garnish with the reserved tomatoes and olives.

Serves 6

Casseroles

There is scarcely a nation in the world that does not have its own regional way of adapting pulses to local conditions, available ingredients and domestic preferences. Mexico has a casserole, now known throughout the Western world, of red kidney beans cooked with chilli and served with rice – the grain constituent that completes the nutritional balance. In France there are many variants of cassoulet, a dish comprising a mixture of meats (chosen from pork, lamb, goose, duck, chicken and spiced sausages) cooked slowly, for a long time, with haricot beans. On Greek islands they cook chick peas overnight with so many vegetables that you forget to look for the meat. North African countries combine chick peas with cous-cous grains around spicy mixtures of meat and vegetable. Neck of lamb cooked with butter beans and bulked up with dumplings is an old British favourite, while the American equivalent is baked beans sweetened with molasses, topped with pork and served with chunks of moist wholewheat bread.

Whichever way you choose to serve them, it is usually best to cook or partly cook the pulses in unsalted stock or water first (at this stage, you can cook extra for salads, fillings and so on). Then add the pulses to the other ingredients to simmer slowly and absorb all the flavours.

Cassoulet

500 g (1 lb) (2²⁄₃ cups) dried white haricot beans, soaked and drained
2.5 litres (4¹⁄₂ pints) (11 cups) unsalted chicken stock
2 large onions, sliced
2 bay leaves
a few stalks of parsley
500 g (1 lb) belly of pork, skinned and diced
500 g (1 lb) (2 cups) chicken meat, diced
250 g (8 oz) (¹⁄₂ lb) chorizo sausage, skinned and sliced
425-g (15-oz) can tomatoes
30 ml (2 tablespoons) tomato purée
10 ml (2 teaspoons) dried oregano
5 ml (1 teaspoon) dried mint
4 cloves garlic, finely chopped
200 g (6 oz) (2 cups) wholewheat breadcrumbs

Cook the beans in the stock with the onions, bay leaves and parsley for 1 hour. Drain the beans, discard the bay leaves and reserve the stock.

In a large casserole, make layers of beans, pork, beans, chicken, beans and sausage. Mix together the reserved stock, tomatoes and the juice from the can, tomato purée, herbs and garlic and pour over the beans. Cover with half the breadcrumbs. Cover and cook in the oven at 150° C, 300° F, Gas 2 for 3½ hours, topping up with more hot stock

if necessary. Push down the breadcrumbs with the back of a spoon, sprinkle on the remainder and cook uncovered for 1 hour more.

Serves 8

Chilli beans

250 g (8 oz) (1¹⁄₄ cups) dried red kidney beans, soaked and drained
30 ml (2 tablespoons) vegetable oil
1 large onion, chopped
2 cloves garlic, crushed
5 ml (1 teaspoon) chilli powder, or to taste
5 ml (1 teaspoon) paprika powder
425-g (15-oz) can tomatoes
15 ml (1 tablespoon) tomato purée
salt

Cook the beans in unsalted, boiling water until they are tender. Heat the oil and fry the onion and garlic over moderate heat for 4 minutes, stirring once or twice. Stir in the chilli powder and paprika for 1 minute. Add the tomatoes, the juice from the can and the tomato purée. Bring to the boil and boil for 5 minutes. Cover and simmer over low heat for 20 minutes. Season with salt.

Chilli beans are good served with rice and green salad for a non-meat meal, or as an accompaniment to roast or grilled meats.

Serves 4

Boston baked beans

350 g (12 oz) (2 cups) dried haricot beans, soaked and drained
15 ml (1 tablespoon) vegetable oil
1 large onion, sliced
250-g (8-oz) can tomatoes
30 ml (2 tablespoons) tomato purée
5 ml (1 teaspoon) mustard powder
15 ml (1 tablespoon) molasses
15 ml (1 tablespoon) molasses sugar
300 ml (½ pint) (1¼ cups) unsalted vegetable or chicken stock
750 g (1½ lb) belly of pork, skinned and sliced
salt and pepper

Cook the beans in unsalted, boiling water until nearly tender; drain. Heat the oil in a flameproof casserole and fry the onion over moderate heat for 4 minutes, stirring once or twice. Add the tomatoes and the juice from the can, tomato purée or mustard, molasses, molasses sugar and stock. Bring to the boil. Arrange the slices of pork on top, cover and cook in the oven at 140° C, 275° F, Gas 1 for 3½–4 hours, stirring occasionally. Season with salt and pepper. Serve with wholewheat bread – steamed brown bread is traditional in New England.

Serves 4

Accompaniments

From large, creamy-white butter beans tossed with herbs to coral-coloured lentil purée piled high, the many different pulses can be served with meat and, to a lesser extent, fish dishes in so many guises that the imagination runs riot. It is just a question of playing mix-and-match with spices and vegetable flavourings. Take butter beans: cook them, then toss them in chopped onions and red peppers spiced with paprika; or in a parsley or onion sauce; or in soured cream topped with crisply fried bacon. Take kidney beans, any kind, and simmer them (after pre-cooking) in a Provençal sauce of tomatoes and herbs; with rice, as they do in Cuba (see recipe), or with chopped vegetables and creamed coconut, in the West Indian way. Take split peas or lentils, cook them with curry spices and top them with sliced banana to make a delicious accompaniment to baked fish – as different as can be from old-fashioned pease pudding (see recipe). Take tiny bright green, shiny mung beans, lightly cook them and toss them in fresh-pea purée for a surprise texture partnership, or aduki beans tossed with rice and crisp and crunchy sesame seeds. In other words, do not worry about what goes with what: just take your pick!

Pease pudding

*500 g (1 lb) (2 cups) yellow split peas,
  soaked and drained*
*1.5 litres (2¾ pints) (7 cups) unsalted
  chicken stock*
2 eggs
50 g (2 oz) (¼ cup) butter
*60 ml (4 tablespoons) (¼ cup) double/
  heavy cream*
2.5 ml (½ teaspoon) sugar
30 ml (2 tablespoons) chopped mint
a large pinch of grated nutmeg
salt and pepper

Tie the peas loosely in a piece of calico or a clean tea-towel. Bring the stock to the boil, immerse the pudding cloth, cover, bring back to the boil and simmer for 2½ hours. Top up with more boiling stock as needed. Sieve the peas into a bowl and beat in the eggs, butter, cream, sugar and mint. Season the mixture with nutmeg, salt and pepper and beat it until smooth. Return it to the rinsed-out cloth, tie the cloth securely, lower it into the boiling stock, cover and boil for a further 30 minutes. Turn out the pudding and serve hot, cut into wedges. Serve with ham, boiled bacon or pork.

Serves 6

Moors and Christians

250 g (8 oz) (1¼ cups) dried black
   beans, soaked and drained
30 ml (2 tablespoons) vegetable oil
1 medium onion, chopped
1 green pepper, seeded and chopped
1 red pepper, seeded and chopped
4 large tomatoes, skinned, seeded and
   chopped
200 g (6 oz) (¾ cup) long-grain brown
   rice
450 ml (¾ pint) (2 cups) chicken or
   vegetable stock
salt and pepper

Cook the beans in boiling, unsalted water
until they are barely tender, then drain
them. Heat the oil and fry the onion and
peppers over moderate heat for 4 minutes,
stirring once or twice. Add the tomatoes, stir
well and simmer until they have formed a
thick paste. Stir in the beans, rice and stock,
season with salt and pepper, cover the pan
and bring to the boil. Simmer for 45–50
minutes, or until the rice is tender and the
stock has been absorbed. Taste and adjust
seasoning if necessary.

   This Cuban dish of pulses and grains is
good with casseroles of lamb and pork, or as
a vegetarian dish with salad.

Serves 4–6

Flageolets with garlic

250 g (8 oz) (1¼ cup) dried flageolets,
   soaked and drained
700 ml (1¼ pints) (3 cups) unsalted
   chicken stock
2 large onions, finely chopped
50 g (2 oz) (¼ cup) butter
6 cloves garlic, finely chopped
salt and pepper
30 ml (2 tablespoons) chopped parsley

Put the beans, stock and one of the onions
into a flameproof casserole, bring to the
boil, cover and cook for 30 minutes. Melt the
butter and fry the remaining onion and the
garlic over moderate heat for 3 minutes. Stir
into the beans, cover and cook in the oven at
150°C, 300°F, Gas 2 for 1 hour. Season
with salt and pepper and stir in the parsley.
Cook for a further 15 minutes.

   Serve with a joint of ham, boiled mutton
or roast leg of lamb.

Serves 4

Indian style

About sixty varieties of lentils alone are used in Indian cooking, so pulses can be seen to rank high in importance, especially among the vegetarian communities. Lentils are cooked and served whole, dry, with each lentil separate, like wheat or rice, or cooked to a purée (see recipe for *dal*) with a variety of spices and flavouring vegetables added. Chopped garlic, chopped fresh ginger, a pinch of asafoetida, grated fresh coconut, tomatoes (though only since the sixteenth century) and even sliced under-ripe plums transform each creamy lentil purée into a dish totally dissimilar from the next. For a dish that is creamier still, you can substitute milk for half the water, beat in 100 g (4 oz) butter to twice the weight of dry lentils and stir in cream or yoghurt just before serving. Lentils can be roasted or deep-fried, dried and served (like nuts) as a savoury snack or to garnish smooth dishes. Soaked but uncooked lentils are ground to a paste with spices and mint leaves, formed into hamburger-sized cakes (*bhalle*) and steamed or deep-fried. Whole peas and beans are cooked with other vegetables and meat in composite dishes, but are usually given more prominence. Cooked chick peas are simmered with red chillis, spice seeds and mint for *channeh sabat*, and black-eyed peas cooked with chillis, cooled and tossed with tamarind in yoghurt are served as a protein-packed salad.

Vegetable curry

*250 g (8 oz) (½ lb) potatoes, peeled and
  diced*
1 small cauliflower, cut into florets
2 medium carrots, thickly sliced
3 small courgettes/zucchini thickly sliced
*60 ml (4 tablespoons) (¼ cup) vegetable
  oil*
1 large onion, sliced
2 cloves garlic, finely chopped
10 ml (2 teaspoons) ground cumin
5 ml (1 teaspoon) ground turmeric
1.5 ml (¼ teaspoon) cayenne
5 ml (1 teaspoon) cumin seeds
250-g (8-oz) can tomatoes
125 g (4 oz) (½ cup) cooked haricot beans
125 g (4 oz) (½ cup) cooked soya beans
*300 ml (½ pint) (1¼ cups) water or
  vegetable stock*
10 ml (2 teaspoons) garam masala
60 ml (4 tablespoons) (¼ cup) cashews
salt and pepper
2 hard-boiled eggs, quartered, to garnish
  SAUCE:
  *300 ml (½ pint) (1¼ cups) plain
    yoghurt*
  1 spring/green onion, thinly sliced
  30 ml (2 tablespoons) chopped mint
  1 clove garlic, crushed
  salt

Partly cook the potatoes, cauliflower, carrots and courgettes/zucchini until they are barely tender. Plunge the vegetables into cold water to cool, then drain. Heat the oil, fry the onion over moderate heat for 4 minutes, stirring once or twice, and stir in the garlic, ground cumin, turmeric, cayenne and cumin seeds. Cook for 1–2 minutes. Add the tomatoes, the juice from the can, the haricot and soya beans and the water or stock. Bring to the boil, cover and simmer for 20 minutes, stirring occasionally.

Stir in the partly cooked vegetables, the garam masala and cashews, season with salt

and pepper and simmer for 5 minutes. Garnish with the egg wedges. Serve with rice and the yoghurt sauce, made by mixing the ingredients into the beaten yoghurt.

Serves 6

Dal

250 g (8 oz) (1 cup) brown Indian lentils,
    washed and drained
900 ml (1½ pints) (3¾ cups) water
2 bay leaves
45 ml (3 tablespoons) vegetable oil
2 large onions, chopped
2 cloves garlic, peeled and crushed
5 ml (1 teaspoon) ground coriander
2.5 ml (½ teaspoon) powdered fenugreek
1.5 ml (¼ teaspoon) ground cumin
2 large ripe tomatoes, skinned, seeded and
    chopped
salt
30 ml (2 tablespoons) chopped coriander
    leaves, if available, or parsley, to garnish

Cook the lentils in the water with the bay leaves for about 1 hour, or until they are tender and the liquid has been absorbed. Cook for a few minutes more over fairly high heat if liquid remains once the pulses are soft. Discard the bay leaves, keeping the mixture warm. While the lentils are cooking, heat the oil and fry the onions, garlic and spices over moderate heat for 5 minutes, stirring frequently. Stir in the tomatoes and cook for 10 minutes, stirring often. Beat the spiced vegetable mixture into the lentils and season with salt. Serve hot, garnished with chopped herbs.

Serves 4

Chapattis

250 g (8 oz) (1½ cups) wholewheat flour
10 ml (2 teaspoons) vegetable oil
150 ml (¼ pint) (⅔ cup) water

Put the flour in a bowl, add the oil and water and mix to a firm dough. Knead on a lightly floured board for 5 minutes. Cover with a damp tea-towel for 2 hours. Knead for a further 5 minutes. Break the dough into pieces the size of a small egg and roll into flat circles about 15 cm (6 inches) across. Heat a heavy-based pan, very lightly brush it with oil and fry the chapattis on both sides until crisp on the outside.

Makes about 8 chapattis

Pies and pasties

Pulses and pastries go well together to make filling, nourishing and tasty portable feasts, equally suitable for picnics and packed lunches. The grain element in the wholewheat flour complements the legumes and results in a snack food that is a first-class protein – ideal for vegetarians. Using wholewheat flour for pastry greatly increases its health value – and its flavour, too. Newcomers to making 'brown' pastry may find it a little difficult to handle the first few times. The trick is to roll it between two sheets of greaseproof paper or foil. To line a flan case, remove the top sheet and, beginning at one edge, loosely wrap the pastry round the rolling-pin. Hold the pin over the flan case and unroll the pastry so that it falls gently into place. No problems!

Samosas

1 small onion, finely chopped
30 ml (2 tablespoons) vegetable oil
2 cloves garlic, crushed
2 green chillis, finely chopped
2 medium courgettes/zucchini, chopped
2.5 ml (1/2 teaspoon) chilli powder, or to taste
2.5 ml (1/2 teaspoon) ground turmeric
175 g (6 oz) (1 cup) cooked dried mung beans
salt
5 ml (1 teaspoon) garam masala
30 ml (2 teaspoons) lemon juice
oil, for deep frying
   PASTRY:
   250 g (8 oz) (1 1/2 cups) 81% wheatmeal self-raising flour
   salt
   25 g (1 oz) (2 tablespoons) butter
   about 75 ml (5 tablespoons) (1/3 cup) water

Fry the onion in the oil for 3–4 minutes, stir in the garlic and chillis and after 2 minutes add the courgettes/zucchini. Fry for 2–3 minutes, then stir in the chilli powder and turmeric. Cook for 1 minute before adding the beans and salt. Simmer over low heat for 10 minutes, stir in the garam masala and lemon juice and cook for 5 minutes more. Stir well and set aside to cool.

For the pastry, sift the flour and salt, tip in the bran and rub in the butter. Sprinkle on the water and mix to a smooth dough. Knead on a lightly floured surface for 10 minutes until the dough is springy. Cover with a damp cloth and set aside for 30 minutes.

Divide the dough into 16 pieces. Roll each one into a 6-cm (4-inch) circle, cut in half and dampen the edges. Spoon the cooled filling on to one end of each pastry piece and fold it over. Press the edges to seal.

Heat oil in a deep pan to 186° C, 360° F, or until a small cube of stale bread turns golden brown in 50 seconds. Deep-fry the samosas a few at a time until they are puffed up and golden. Drain them on kitchen paper. Eat hot or cold.

Makes 32 small samosas

Lentil and tomato pasties/pie

1 large onion, chopped
25 g (1 oz) (2 tablespoons) margarine
1 clove garlic, crushed
175 g (6 oz) (3/4 cup) red lentils, washed and drained
300 ml (1/2 pint) (1 1/4 cups) unsalted chicken or vegetable stock
2 large tomatoes, skinned and chopped
5 ml (1 teaspoon) dried oregano
5 ml (1 teaspoon) Worcestershire sauce
salt and pepper
125 g (4 oz) (1 cup) Cheddar cheese, grated

WHOLEWHEAT SHORTCRUST PASTRY:

250 g (8 oz) (1⅓ cups) wholewheat
   flour
salt
75 g (3 oz) (⅓ cup) margarine
50 g (2 oz) (¼ cup) butter
30–45 ml (2–3 tablespoons) water
1 egg, beaten

To make the filling, fry the onion in the margarine for 3–4 minutes. Add the garlic and lentils, stir well and pour on the stock. Bring to the boil, cover and simmer for 30 minutes. Add the tomatoes, oregano and sauce and season with salt and pepper. Bring to the boil and simmer, uncovered, until the mixture is dry. Remove from the heat. Stir in the cheese and cool.

To make the pastry, sift the flour and salt, tip in the bran from the sieve and rub in the margarine and butter until the mixture is like fine crumbs. Make a firm dough with the water and knead lightly.

Roll out on a lightly floured board and cut into 15-cm (6-inch) circles. Spoon the filling on to one half of each circle and brush the edge with water or milk. Fold over the pastry to enclose the filling, pinch together the edges, and brush the tops with beaten egg. Place on a baking sheet and bake in the oven at 200°C, 400°F, Gas 6 for 10 minutes. Lower the heat to 190°C, 375°F, Gas 5 and cook for a further 10–15 minutes. Serve warm or cold.

Makes 6

Alternatively, line a greased 20-cm (8-inch) flan tin with pastry, cover with the cooled filling and then with a pastry lid. Decorate the top and bake in the oven at 200°C, 400°F, Gas 6 for 35–40 minutes.

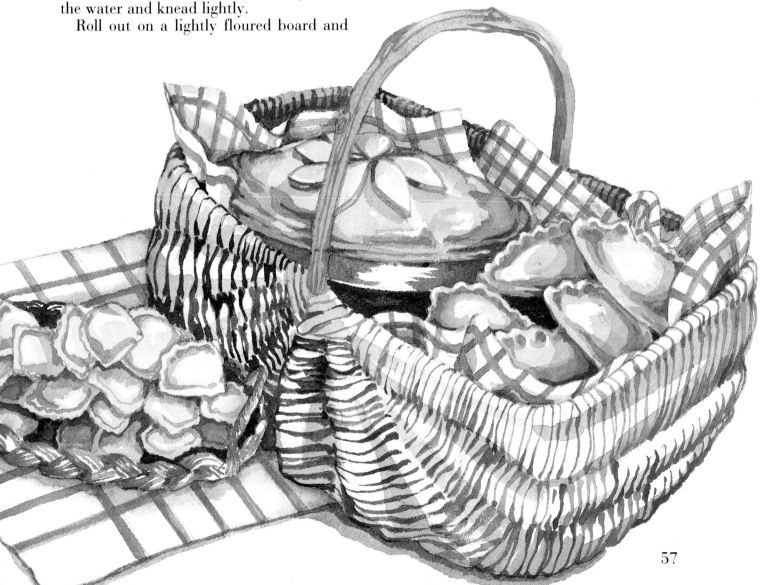

GRAINS

Cereals, or grains, were named after the Roman goddess of the harvest, Ceres. They are the edible seeds of plants cultivated from grasses and include wheat, corn, oats, barley, rye, rice and millet and buckwheat. Throughout history, every civilization has depended on the grain that grows most readily in the local soil and climate – rice in China, Japan and India, wheat predominant in the West, with the hardier cereals, oats, barley and rye, grown in cold northern conditions, and corn, that most golden of harvests, across America. All these cereals are ground into flour but only wheat has the high gluten content necessary to make a light, well-risen loaf. For that reason other flours are usually mixed with a proportion of wheat to facilitate raising. Whole grains may be cooked and served as a main dish or accompaniment, cracked grains – bulghar for example – soaked and eaten raw as a salad, and rolled and flaked grains such as oats eaten raw as a breakfast cereal.

Wheat

Just by switching from white to wholewheat flour (wholemeal and wholegrain are synonyms) for all bread, pastry, cakes, biscuits/cookies and sauces, you can make a considerable contribution to a healthy diet. Each grain of wheat is made up of three parts. Around the outside is the skin or husk, which consists of dietary fibre and is known as bran. Inside that, and comprising about 90 per cent of the grain, is the endosperm, which is largely starch. It is the small speck of the grain, the germ, which contains the nutrients – vitamins of the B group, vitamin E, calcium, potassium, iron, copper, magnesium and fat. When grain is milled to make white flour from the starchy endosperm alone, both the bran and wheatgerm are extracted – and their health-giving properties with them. Both bran and wheatgerm are sold separately and can be added to flours and cereals of all kinds (see bread recipe). Rolled wheat flakes are used mainly in muesli. Plain wholewheat flour has no additives; self-raising flour is marketed with sifted-in raising agents – or you can of course add them yourself. You can also buy 85 per cent and 81 per cent wheatmeal flours. The percentage relates to the extraction rate of bran removed in the milling, 15 and 19 per cent respectively. There are two points to note. First, wholewheat flours, containing the germ, have a short shelf-life – the vitamin E and fat content deteriorate after a few weeks. For the same reason, 'loose' wheatgerm (unless stabilized) must be stored in the refrigerator. And secondly, don't say 'brown', say 'wholewheat': brown flour may be nothing better than coloured white flour.

Whole wheat grains can be cooked and served like rice. Simmer the grain in 3 times its volume of stock or water (1 cup wheat, 3 cups liquid) for 1 hour. Or soak the wheat in the liquid overnight, bring to the boil and simmer for 30 minutes.

Cracked, crushed or kibbled wheat is the whole grain coarsely ground. You can add it to bread and cake mixtures or sprinkle it on top for extra crunch. To cook, simmer in 2½ times its volume of stock or water for 20 minutes.

Bulghar or burgul is made by soaking whole wheat grains and roasting them until they crack. It can be soaked and served without further cooking as a salad (see recipe). To cook, simmer in twice its volume of stock or water for 15 minutes.

Mushroom and pepper pizza

1 large green pepper
1 large red pepper
1 large onion, chopped
2 cloves garlic, finely chopped
30 ml (2 tablespoons) vegetable oil
250-g (8-oz) can tomatoes
30 ml (2 tablespoons) tomato purée
10 ml (2 teaspoons) dried oregano
salt and pepper
150 g (5 oz) mozzarella cheese, thinly
  sliced
250 g (8 oz) (½ lb) button mushrooms,
  thinly sliced
  SCONE DOUGH:
  250 g (8 oz) (1½ cups) wholewheat
    flour
  15 ml (1 tablespoon) baking powder
  salt
  50 g (2 oz) (½ cup) medium
    oatmeal
  2.5 ml (½ teaspoon) dried basil
  50 g (2 oz) (¼ cup) margarine
  1 egg
  45 ml (3 tablespoons) milk

Trim the peppers and remove the seeds. Slice half of each pepper into thin rings and set aside. Chop the remainder. Fry the onion, garlic and chopped pepper in the oil for 4 minutes over moderate heat, stirring often. Tip in the can of tomatoes, add the tomato purée and oregano and season with salt and pepper. Bring to the boil and simmer, uncovered, for 20–25 minutes, or until the mixture forms a thick paste. Adjust seasoning if needed. Set aside to cool.

Sift together the flour, baking powder and salt, tip in the bran from the sieve and stir in the oatmeal and basil. Rub in the margarine. Beat together the egg and milk and mix into the dry ingredients. Form into a dough and knead lightly. Roll out on a lightly floured board to a 25-cm (10-inch) circle and place on a baking sheet.

Spread the tomato paste over the pizza base. Cover with the cheese slices, then arrange the pepper rings and mushroom slices. Bake in the oven at 200°C, 400°F, Gas 6 for 35 minutes. Serve warm.

Serves 6

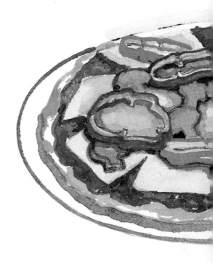

Bulghar salad

250 g (8 oz) (1½ cup) bulghar wheat
12 spring/green onions, finely chopped
60 ml (4 tablespoons) (¼ cup) chopped
  mint
60 ml (4 tablespoons) (¼ cup) chopped
  parsley
2 cloves garlic, crushed
90 ml (6 tablespoons) (⅓ cup) olive oil
30 ml (2 tablespoons) lemon juice
salt and pepper
1 cucumber, thinly sliced
4 large, firm tomatoes, quartered, to
  garnish
12 black olives to garnish

Soak the wheat in cold water for 30 minutes. Drain it, turn it into a clean tea-towel and squeeze it dry. Mix the wheat with the onions, herbs, garlic, oil and lemon juice and season well with salt and pepper. Arrange cucumber slices around a dish, pile the salad in the centre and garnish with the tomatoes and olives. Serve with hard-boiled eggs, cold meats or other salad dishes.

Serves 4

Wheatgerm bread

500 g (1 lb) (3 cups) wholewheat flour
50 g (2 oz) (¾ cup) wheatgerm
50 g (2 oz) (1¼ cups) bran
5 ml (1 teaspoon) salt
10 ml (2 teaspoons) bicarbonate of soda
5 ml (1 teaspoon) dark muscovado/brown
  sugar
60 g (2½ oz) (⅓ cup) butter
300 ml (½ pint) (1¼ cups) buttermilk or
  soured milk
45 ml (3 tablespoons) cracked wheat

Mix together the flour, wheatgerm, bran, salt, soda and sugar and rub in the butter. Pour on the buttermilk or soured milk and mix to form a dough. Knead on a lightly floured board. Place in a greased 900-g (2-lb) loaf-tin, sprinkle with the topping and bake in the oven at 200° C, 400° F, Gas 6 for 45 minutes.

Makes one 20-cm (8-inch) loaf

Corn

Sweetcorn, or maize, native to Central America, is enjoyable in many forms. The whole ears of corn may be boiled, roasted or grilled. Stripped from the corn the kernels can be cooked in chowders (see recipe) casseroles, soup – with plenty of onions and cream – and gratinated dishes. Once cooked, the kernels can be stirred into a batter to make fry-on-the-griddle breakfast corncakes, or into the sauce that forms the basis of high-rise soufflés. Kernels are available frozen and are sold in cans.

Cornmeal, the early staple flour of America, was used in breads with the most romantic of names – johnnycake, ash bread, spoonbread and cracklin' bread. The meal has low rising properties and lighter breads are achieved by combining it with wheat flour (see recipe). Cornmeal can be yellow or white, and finely or coarsely ground. *Polenta* is the Italian equivalent and *masa harina* is the Mexican version, used for *tortillas* and *taco* shells, in which the corn kernels are treated with lime before grinding. Store cornmeals in airtight containers in a cool, dry place for up to 2 months. Cornflour, or cornstarch, is a very fine, and refined, powder used mainly for thickening.

Hominy, sold ready-cooked in cans, is the large, cooked, starchy endosperm of the hulled maize kernel, served to accompany meat. Hominy grits, or just 'grits', are coarsely ground and used to make a type of porridge.

Popcorn is a variety of corn that 'explodes' when heated. Add 125 g (4 oz) (½ cup) popping corn to 15 ml (1 tablespoon) vegetable oil in a large pan, shake over moderate heat and hold on the lid tightly. In seconds the corn will be ready to serve.

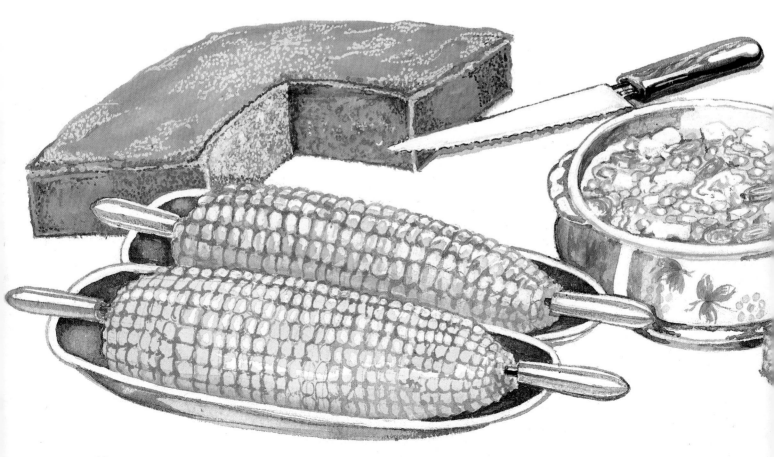

Roast sweetcorn

4 young ears of sweetcorn
salt and pepper
40 g (1½ oz) (3 tablespoons) butter,
*   softened*
*   PARSLEY BUTTER:*
50 g (2 oz) (¼ cup) butter, softened
1 clove garlic, crushed
5 ml (1 teaspoon) lemon juice
45 ml (3 tablespoons) chopped parsley

Strip the husk and silk from the corn and trim the ends. Place each one on a square of buttered foil and divide the softened butter between them. Season well with salt and pepper and close the foil, sealing the joins tightly. Cook on a rack in the oven at 200°C, 400°F, Gas 6 for 20 minutes. Open the foil and arrange pats of herb butter on top. Serve at once, with a toothpick 'spear' in each end.

To make the herb butter, beat the butter and garlic, then gradually beat in the lemon juice, drop by drop. Beat in the parsley, shape into a roll, wrap in foil and chill. The herb butter will keep for several weeks.

Serves 4

Note *Alternatively, cook the ears of corn ranch-style over a barbecue for 20 minutes, turning often.*

Cornbread

250 g (8 oz) (1½ cups) wholewheat flour
15 ml (1 tablespoon) baking powder
5 ml (1 teaspoon) salt
175 g (6 oz) (1 cup) cornmeal
50 g (2 oz) (¼ cup) light muscovado/
*   brown sugar*
200 ml (7 fl oz) (⅞ cup) plain yoghurt
45 ml (3 tablespoons) milk
1 egg
25 g (1 oz) (2 tablespoons) butter, melted
*   and cooled*

Sift together the flour, baking powder and salt, tip in the bran and stir in the cornmeal and sugar. Mix together the yoghurt, milk, egg and butter and stir into the dry ingredients. Mix to a dough. Turn the mixture into a greased 20-cm (8-in) square baking tin and bake in the oven at 220°C, 425°F, Gas 7 for 20 minutes. If possible, serve the bread warm, cut in squares and buttered.

Makes one 20-cm (8-inch) loaf

Fish and corn chowder

500 g (1 lb) fillet of haddock or cod
600 ml (1 pint) (2½ cups) water
salt and pepper
1 bouquet garni
½ lemon, sliced
2 ears of sweetcorn
250 g (8 oz) (½ lb) potatoes, diced
1 medium leek, sliced
2.5 ml (½ teaspoon) mustard powder
300 ml (½ pint) (1¼ cups) single/light
*   cream*
45 ml (3 tablespoons) chopped parsley

Poach the fish in the water with salt, pepper, the bouquet garni and lemon for 10 minutes. Remove the fish, skin it, remove any bones and cut it into 5-cm (2-inch) pieces. Discard the herbs and lemon.

Using a sharp knife, strip the kernels from the sweetcorn heads. Cook the potatoes and corn kernels in the fish stock for 10 minutes. Add the leek and mustard powder and cook for 8–10 minutes, until the vegetables are just tender. Return the fish to the pan, stir in cream and re-heat gently. Adjust the seasoning. Serve, sprinkled with parsley, with masses of hot, crusty wholewheat bread.

Serves 4

Oats

For centuries a bowl of porridge – a particular favourite in Scotland – was considered an ample and healthy start to the day, and now oats in another form, as the main ingredient in muesli, are taking over. Recipes for both are given here – take your choice. Whole oats are good news. They contain more protein and thiamine than any rival grain, significant amounts of iron and potassium, and little fat. Whole oat grains, or groats, can be cooked like wheat, as a pilaff or accompaniment. Oats are ground to three grades of meal, the coarsest being pin-head oats, which need overnight soaking before long, slow cooking. Medium and fine oatmeal can be used for oatcakes, biscuits/cookies and bannocks and mixed with wheat flour in breads, scones and cakes: oatmeal alone has insufficient gluten to rise successfully. Rolled oat flakes are made from whole oats (when they are called jumbo oats) and from the pin-head type. They are the traditional cereal for flapjacks and treacle tart and they, too, can be mixed with wholewheat flour in bread, scones and pastry. Oat bran and oat germ, the outer husk and the embryo of the grain, are sold, packaged together, as a healthy cereal additive.

Porridge

*125 g (4 oz) (1 cup) medium oatmeal,
  soaked overnight and drained*
*25 g (1 oz) (¼ cup) oat bran and oat
  germ*
600 ml (1 pint) (2½ cups) boiling water
salt

Sprinkle the oatmeal, bran and germ on to the boiling water. Return to the boil, stirring constantly, and simmer gently over very low heat for 20 minutes, stirring frequently. Stir in the salt and serve at once. Serve with plain yoghurt, milk or honey to taste, and add dried fruits for extra sweetness and fibre.

Serves 4

Granola

225 g (8 oz) (2²/3 cups) rolled oat flakes
125 g (4 oz) (1¹/3 cups) wheat flakes
125 g (4 oz) (1¹/3 cups) barley flakes
50 g (2 oz) (¹/2 cup) sunflower seeds
25 g (1 oz) (3 tablespoons) millet seeds
50 g (2 oz) (¹/3 cup) sesame seeds
*225 g (8 oz) (2 cups) mixed nuts (can be
    broken ones)*
75 g (3 oz) (1 cup) shredded coconut
125 g (4 oz) (¹/3 cup) clear honey
*50 g (2 oz) (¹/4 cup) light muscovado/
    brown sugar*
45 ml (3 tablespoons) vegetable oil
225 g (8 oz) (1¹/3 cups) seedless raisins

Mix together the oats, flakes, seeds, nuts and coconut. Melt the honey, sugar and oil, pour over the dry ingredients and mix well. Spread on baking trays. Cook in the oven at 160°C, 325°F, Gas 3 for 25 minutes, stirring often. Cool completely, then stir in the raisins. Store in an airtight container. Serve with plain yoghurt, milk, buttermilk or fruit juice.

Makes 1.1 kg (2¹/2 lb)

Note *Stir in other dried vine fruits and nuts instead of, or as well as, the raisins.*

Muesli

225 g (8 oz) (2²/3 cups) rolled oat flakes
175 g (6 oz) (2 cups) rolled wheat flakes
175 g (6 oz) (2 cups) rolled rye flakes
175 g (6 oz) (2 cups) rolled barley flakes
125 g (4 oz) (³/4 cup) sunflower seeds
125 g (4 oz) (1 cup) hazelnuts, chopped
*125 g (4 oz) (³/4 cup) compressed dates,
    chopped*
*125 g (4 oz) (³/4 cup) dried apricots,
    chopped*
50 g (2 oz) (²/3 cup) dried prune flakes
125 g (4 oz) (²/3 cup) seedless raisins

Mix all the ingredients together and store in an airtight container. Serve with fresh fruits such as grated apple, strawberries or orange segments, according to season, and with plain yoghurt, buttermilk, milk or fruit juices.

Makes 1.25 kg (2³/4 lb)

Note 1 *This is only a starting point in making your own muesli. The grains, nuts and fruits are infinitely variable.*
Note 2 *For a savoury alternative, omit the dried apricots and prune flakes and serve the muesli with vegetables such as grated carrots, thinly sliced mushrooms, celery and fennel. Savoury muesli is best with yoghurt.*

Oatcakes

*225 g (8 oz) (2 cups) medium oatmeal,
    plus extra for topping*
50 g (2 oz) (¹/3 cup) wholewheat flour
5 ml (1 teaspoon) baking powder
50 g (2 oz) (¹/4 cup) margarine, melted
*about 45–60 ml (3–4 tablespoons) boiling
    water*

Mix together the oatmeal, flour and baking powder and stir in the melted margarine. Mix to a firm dough with the boiling water. Knead on a lightly floured board and roll to 6 mm (¹/4 inch) thick. Cut into 6-cm (2¹/2-inch) rounds and place on a baking sheet. Sprinkle the tops with a little extra oatmeal. Bake in the oven at 190°C, 375°F, Gas 5 for 10–12 minutes. Transfer to a wire rack to cool.

Makes about 16

Barley

Tennyson wrote of the 'long fields of barley and of rye' running down to Camelot. Both cereals can survive in climates too cold to grow wheat, and were staples in northern countries. Barley flour has a low gluten content and does not rise in baking (in the Middle Ages the hard, flat, biscuit-like loaves were used as plates); it has a nutty flavour and can successfully be mixed half-and-half with wheat flour. Pot barley is the grain with the tough outer husk removed – the equivalent of whole wheat, but paler in colour. Cook it in boiling water for 1¼–1½ hours. Pearl barley, used to thicken soups and stews, cooks in about 25 minutes. Not only the husk but the outer layers of the grain are processed out to obtain the chalky white appearance. This is the form used to make barley water.

Rye

This was the staple grain of many parts of Eastern and Northern Europe until the mid-nineteenth century, when more hardy varieties of wheat were raised. Rye flour is mixed in roughly equal quantities with wholewheat flour, much higher in gluten, for bread with the pleasant sour taste of rye and the characteristic lightness of wheat baking. Rye bread is specially good with continental sausages, cream cheese and sour pickles such as dill cucumbers. The whole grains, darkish brown in colour, can be cooked for pilaffs and 'vegetable' accompaniments and take about 1¼ hours to soften. 'Cracked rye' is the whole cereal crushed to make it easier to cook. Boil for 15 minutes, then set aside for 5 minutes before serving. Toss in herb butter (page 63).

Rye baps

25 g (1 oz) (2 packets) fresh yeast or 15 g
  (½ oz) (2 packets) dried yeast
5 ml (1 teaspoon) light muscovado/brown
  sugar
150 ml (¼ pint) (⅔ cup) warm water
250 g (8 oz) (1½ cups) rye flour, plus extra
  for topping
250 g (8 oz) (1½ cups) wholewheat flour
10 ml (2 teaspoons) salt
40 g (1½ oz) (3 tablespoons) butter
150 ml (¼ pint) (⅔ cup) warm milk
1 egg, beaten

Cream together the fresh yeast, sugar and
water. For dried yeast, mix together the
sugar and water and sprinkle the yeast on
top. Set either yeast mixture aside in a warm
place for 10 minutes until it is frothy. Stir
together the flours and salt and rub in the
butter. Pour in the yeast mixture and the
milk and mix to a dough. Knead on a lightly
floured surface for about 10 minutes, until
the dough is pliable. Cover with a damp
cloth and leave in a warm place to rise for
about 1 hour. It should double in bulk.

Knead the dough again for 5 minutes.
Divide into 12 equal pieces, shape each one
into a ball and roll to about 6 mm (¼ inch)
thick. Place on a floured baking sheet, cover
and leave to rise for 10 minutes. Brush the
tops with beaten egg and sprinkle with rye
flour. Bake in the oven at 200°C, 400°F,
Gas 6 for 20–25 minutes. Cool on a wire
rack and dust with more flour.

Makes 12

Barley vegetable pilaff

250 g (8 oz) (1 cup) pot barley
1 large onion, chopped
2 cloves garlic, crushed
30 ml (2 tablespoons) vegetable oil
125 g (4 oz) (¼ lb) small button
  mushrooms, sliced
3 small courgettes/zucchini, sliced
5 ml (1 teaspoon) dried oregano
2 medium cooked carrots, diced
45 ml (3 tablespoons) orange juice
75 g (3 oz) (¾ cup) mixed nuts
60 ml (4 tablespoons) (¼ cup) dried
  mulberries or sultanas
salt and pepper
30 ml (2 tablespoons) chopped chives to
  garnish
grated cheese to serve

Cook the pot barley in plenty of boiling
water for 1–1¼ hours, or until it is just
tender; drain. Fry the onion and garlic in the
oil for 4–5 minutes over moderate heat,
stirring once or twice. Stir in the
mushrooms, courgettes/zucchini and
oregano and simmer, covered, over low heat
for 5 minutes. Stir in the barley, carrots and
orange juice and simmer for 5 minutes
more. Stir in the nuts and dried fruit, season
with salt and pepper and garnish with the
chives. Serve hot, handing the grated cheese
separately. The pilaff makes a filling
informal meal with cheese and salad, or may
accompany meat.

Serves 4–6

Rice

Nutritionally, as with wheat, there is a world of difference between brown and white rice. Much of the protein, B vitamins, phosphorus, potassium, iron, calcium and dietary fibre – not to mention the delicious, almost nutty flavours – are milled out when rice is refined and polished. Brown rice takes longer to cook – 40–45 minutes – but more easily produces good results. Choose the short-grain type when separated grains are important to the 'finish' of the dish, as for pilaffs, polos, salads and as an accompaniment – and for puddings. Brown long-grain rice comes into its own when it is cooked and served in liquid, as in soups, stews and casseroles.

There are two main methods of cooking, boiling in plenty of water or steaming in a measured amount. To boil rice for 4 people, add 250 g (8 oz) (1 cup) rice to a large pan of boiling, salted water, stir once, lower the heat, cover and simmer for 40–45 minutes, until the grains are just tender. Drain in a colander, refresh in cold water and drain again. Toss in butter or herb butter, yoghurt or soured cream.

To steam the rice, heat 30 ml (2 tablespoons) vegetable oil in a pan, stir in 250 g (8 oz) (1 cup) rice and pour on 600 ml (1 pint) (2 cups) hot vegetable or chicken stock or water. Stir once, cover, lower the heat and simmer for 45 minutes without removing the lid. Stir with a fork, 'glaze' as suggested, and leave the rice to rest in a warm place for 5–10 minutes before serving.

This is the way to start savoury pilaffs, adding onions, garlic, herbs, spices and nuts for flavouring.

Fruit, vegetable, nut and rice salad

1 green pepper, halved and seeded
1 red pepper, halved and seeded
125 g (4 oz) (³/₄ cup) cooked short-grain
  brown rice
4 large, firm tomatoes, seeded and
  quartered
2 cloves garlic, crushed
125 g (4 oz) (²/₃ cup) cooked sweetcorn·
  kernels
125 g (4 oz) (¹/₄ lb) button mushrooms,
  thinly sliced
125 g (4 oz) (²/₃ cup) seedless raisins
125 g (4 oz) (³/₄ cup) fresh or dried dates,
  stoned and chopped
125 g (4 oz) (1 cup) mixed nuts, roughly
  chopped
125 g (4 oz) (³/₄ cup) seedless green grapes
60 ml (4 tablespoons) (¹/₄ cup) black olives
  DRESSING:
  300 ml (¹/₂ pint) (1¹/₄ cups) plain
    yoghurt, chilled
  grated rind and juice of 1 orange
  salt and pepper
  salad leaves to serve

Grill the peppers, skin-side-up, for 5 minutes. Skin them and cut into strips. Mix together the rice, all the vegetables, fruit, nuts and olives, cover and chill in the refrigerator.

Mix together the yoghurt, orange rind and juice and season lightly with salt and pepper. Pour over the salad and toss well. Serve on a bed of salad leaves.

Serves 6–8

Lamb polo

This dish, combining rice, lamb and dried fruits, is similar to pilaff but arranged in layers. The rice finishes cooking by steaming.

175 g (6 oz) (³/₄ cup) short-grain brown
  rice
salt
15 ml (1 tablespoon) vegetable oil
1 large onion, chopped
500 g (1 lb) lean lamb, cut into 2.5-cm
  (1-inch) cubes
125 g (4 oz) (³/₄ cup) dried apricots,
  quartered
50 g (2 oz) (¹/₃ cup) sultanas
2.5 ml (¹/₂ teaspoon) ground ginger
5 ml (1 teaspoon) ground turmeric
10 ml (2 teaspoons) cumin seeds
pepper
600 ml (1 pint) (2¹/₂ cups) hot chicken
  stock
50 g (2 oz) (¹/₄ cup) butter, softened

Cook the rice in salted water for 30–35 minutes, until nearly tender. Drain, refresh in cold water, drain and leave to cool. Heat the oil and fry the onion over moderate heat for 3–4 minutes, stirring once or twice. Add the lamb and stir to seal on all sides. Add the apricots, sultanas and spices, season with salt and pepper, stir well and cook for 1 minute. Pour on the stock, bring to the boil and simmer gently, covered, for 1¹/₄ hours, or until the meat is tender. Use the butter to grease a flame-proof casserole. Make a 12-mm (¹/₂-inch) layer of rice, then continue making layers of meat and rice, finishing with the grain. Place a double layer of foil over the rice, then cover with a lid. Steam over very low heat for 20 minutes, or until the rice is tender and has absorbed the sauce.

Serve with chutneys and poppadoms.

Serves 6

Note *Make a rice polo with other spiced mixtures too – chicken, beef or vegetable medleys such as carrots, tomatoes and courgettes/zucchini.*

Buckwheat, sorghum and cous-cous

The name buckwheat comes from the Dutch *book-weit*, beech nut, the seeds being a similar triangular shape. They are the seeds of a plant in the rhubarb family (therefore not a true grain) and a staple food in Russia. There they are known as *kasha*, which also describes the strong nutty-tasting porridge made with them. Buckwheat is high in protein, phosphorus and potassium and has most of the B vitamins. The grains have a relatively short cooking time, about 12–15 minutes. Toasted buckwheat, which has been lightly roasted, is sold ready to eat. Add it to muesli or to give a crunchy texture to baked goods. Japanese *soba* noodles are made from buckwheat flour. *Blinis*, the Russian yeast-raised pancakes, are traditionally served with caviar and soured cream.

Sorghum may be cooked in the same way as rice, wheat and other groats for use in pilaffs and casseroles, added to soups, incorporated in salads, and so on. Sorghum flour, milled from the whole grain, is gluten-free and therefore produces only flat bread. It is best mixed with high-gluten flour such as wholewheat for baked goods. Sorghum is high in nutrients and also in fat, and so has a short shelf-life. Store in the refrigerator.

Cous-cous pellets, or grains, are produced from semolina, a product of hard durum wheat, and made commercially by moistening the semolina grains, coating them in a fine flour and 'expanding' them. In North Africa the cereal is a national accompaniment to meat, fish and vegetable dishes. Steamed cous-cous is a good accompaniment to curry, and can be served hot or cold as a dessert, sweetened with honey, maple syrup and dried fruits.

Buckwheat blinis

5 ml (1 teaspoon) light muscovado/brown
 sugar
600 ml (1 pint) (2½ cups) warm milk
10 ml (2 teaspoons) dried yeast
250 g (8 oz) (1½ cups) buckwheat flour,
250 g (8 oz) (1½ cups) wholewheat flour
salt
2 eggs, separated
40 g (1½ oz) (3 tablespoons) butter,
 melted
oil for frying

Have all the utensils warm, at room
temperature. Mix the sugar with 60 ml (4
tablespoons) (¼ cup) of the milk and
sprinkle on the yeast. Stir well and leave in a
warm place for 10 minutes. Sift together the
flours and salt and tip in the bran. Add the
yeast mixture and the remainder of the milk
alternately with the flour. Beat in the egg
yolks one at a time, then the melted butter.
Whisk the egg whites until stiff and fold
them into the butter. Cover and leave in a
warm place for about 30 minutes, until
doubled in bulk.

Heat a heavy-based frying-pan and
lightly brush with oil. Drop in 45 ml (3
tablespoons) of the batter and cook over
moderate heat for 3 minutes, until bubbles
appear on the surface. Toss or flip over and
cook the second side for 2–3 minutes. Keep
the *blinis* warm on a foil-covered dish over a
pan of simmering water.

Serve with lumpfish roe ('poor man's
caviar'), soured cream and lemon wedges.

Makes about 12

Cous-cous

500 g (1 lb) (2⅔ cups) cous-cous grains
225 ml (8 fl oz) (1 cup) water
25 g (1 oz) (2 tablespoons) butter
30 ml (2 tablespoons) olive oil
salt and pepper

Put the cous-cous grains into a bowl and
sprinkle on a third of the water. Mix well.
Line a colander with a clean, scalded
tea-towel. Sprinkle half the remaining water
on to the now sticky cous-cous and stir well
to separate the grains. Tip the cous-cous
into the colander and fit it over a pan with a
little boiling water. Fold the cloth over the
cous-cous and steam for 30 minutes, stirring
occasionally. Tip the cous-cous into a bowl
and sprinkle on the remaining water. Stir in
the butter and oil and season well with salt
and pepper. Now place the bowl over the
pan of boiling water, cover the grains with a
cloth and steam for a further 30 minutes,
stirring occasionally.

Serve with a mixture of steamed or
simmered vegetables, such as onions,
carrots, celery, cauliflower, courgettes/
zucchini, mushrooms, tomatoes and peas –
about 900 g (2 lb) in all. A sauce of tomatoes
and pimentos spiced with cumin, coriander
and paprika is traditional.

Arrange the cous-cous around a serving
dish, pile the vegetables over the sauce or
serve it separately.

Serves 6

PASTA

Just as its name indicates, pasta is a paste or type of pastry, made from semolina grains milled from Canadian or American hard durum wheat and formed into a bewildering variety of shapes. It is thought to have been invented by the Chinese 6,000 years ago and brought to Italy, considerably later, by Marco Polo. In some speciality shops and delicatessens you can buy fresh pasta – soft, pliable, full of flavour, and taking only about 5 minutes to cook. And given time, you can make it yourself at home. By far the greatest quantity of pasta, however, is bought dried and packaged, and with a conveniently long shelf-life: in an airtight container you can store it in a cool, dry place for up to six months. There are four main types: wholewheat, made from the whole grain; 'standard' pasta, made from only the endosperm; the green (*verdi*) type, which has spinach added to the semolina; and buckwheat pasta, made from the whole buckwheat seed.

There is an ever-growing pasta industry in both the United States and Great Britain; much of the buckwheat pasta is imported from Japan. Whether you choose 'elbow' macaroni, folded *tagliatelle*, large *conchiglie* shells, long spaghetti, the quill-shaped *penne*, *farfalle* (bows) or large *rigatoni* tubes (from left to right in the illustration), pasta offers healthy variety.

Pasta is food-value

Pasta has acquired a bad name from the health-food standpoint – not because of what it is, but because of what we tend to put with it: oil, butter, cream, cheese and all the other high-calorie and animal-fat accompaniments. Wholewheat and buckwheat pasta, made from the whole grain, are high in dietary fibre. Wholewheat pasta has a minimum fibre content of 10 per cent, with 13 per cent protein and 2.8 per cent fat, and is available in an increasing variety of shapes including spaghetti, macaroni, shells, wheels and lasagne. Standard pasta – in common with white bread and polished rice – is appreciably lower in fibre at 0.3 per cent, with 14 per cent protein and about 1.2 per cent fat. The spinach pasta types vary little in analysis from the standard kind.

Spinach and pasta moulds

175 g (6 oz) (1½ cups) wholewheat
short-cut macaroni
salt
50 g (2 oz) (¼ cup) margarine
1 small onion, finely chopped
250 g (8 oz) (½ lb) spinach, chopped
100 g (4 oz) (1 cup) hazelnuts, ground
2 eggs, beaten
pepper
a pinch of grated nutmeg

Cook the macaroni in plenty of boiling, salted water for 10–12 minutes, until it is just tender. Drain, rinse and drain again. Melt the margarine and fry the onion for 3–4 minutes, stirring once or twice. Add the spinach and stir until it collapses. Simmer for 5 minutes, then drain very thoroughly. Mix together the macaroni, spinach, 75 g (3 oz) (¾ cup) of the nuts and the eggs and season with salt, pepper and nutmeg.

Turn the mixture into 6 greased dariole moulds or into a greased pudding basin lined with the remaining ground nuts. Tightly cover with foil and steam over boiling water for 45 minutes (small moulds) to 1 hour. Serve hot, with tomato sauce.

Serves 4

Pasta and Roquefort salad

125 g (4 oz) (1⅔ cup) wholewheat pasta
shells
salt
50 g (2 oz) (½ cup) walnut halves
3 tender stalks celery, thinly sliced
2 dessert apples, cored and thinly sliced
50 g (2 oz) (½ cup) Roquefort cheese,
crumbled
30 ml (2 tablespoons) chopped chives
DRESSING:
45 ml (3 tablespoons) vegetable oil
30 ml (2 tablespoons) orange juice
pepper

Cook the pasta shells in boiling, salted water for about 12 minutes, until they are just tender. Drain, rinse in cold water and drain again. Mix together the oil and orange juice for the dressing, season with pepper and toss in the hot pasta. Cool. Toss in the walnuts, celery, apples, cheese and chives. Serve with green and other salads, or with cold poultry or meats.

Serves 4

Buckwheat spaghetti with prawn sauce

50 g (2 oz) (¼ cup) butter
1 medium onion, finely chopped
1 large clove garlic, crushed
500 g (1 lb) courgettes/zucchini, sliced
10 ml (2 teaspoons) dried basil
4 large tomatoes, skinned and quartered
    pepper
350 g (12 oz) (¾ lb) cooked, shelled
    prawns
45 ml (3 tablespoons) black olives
350 g (12 oz) (¾ lb) buckwheat spaghetti
salt
15 ml (1 tablespoon) chopped chives
15 ml (1 tablespoon) chopped parsley
grated Parmesan cheese to serve

Melt half the butter, fry the onion and garlic for 3–4 minutes, add the courgettes/zucchini and stir well. Cook over low heat for 5 minutes, stir in the basil and tomatoes and cook for 5 minutes more. Season with salt and pepper, stir in the prawns and olives and heat through.

Cook the spaghetti in plenty of boiling, salted water for about 12–15 minutes, until just tender. Drain, rinse, drain again and toss with the remaining butter.

Turn the spaghetti on to a heated dish, pour the sauce over and sprinkle on the fresh herbs. Serve with the cheese and a green salad.

Serves 4

Tomato sauce

1 medium onion, finely chopped
1 clove garlic, crushed
30 ml (2 tablespoons) vegetable oil
450-g (15-oz) can tomatoes
15 ml (1 tablespoon) tomato purée
5 ml (1 teaspoon) dried oregano, basil or
    thyme
salt and pepper

Fry the onion and garlic in the oil for 4–5 minutes over moderate heat, stirring occasionally. Tip in the tomatoes and juice, add the purée and herbs and bring to the boil. Simmer, uncovered, for about 1 hour, or until the sauce has thickened. Season with salt and pepper. For a little piquancy, add about 5 ml (1 teaspoon) Worcestershire sauce and up to 5 ml (1 teaspoon) dark muscovado/brown sugar.

The sauce freezes well, so it is worth making it in larger quantities.

Serves 4

Cooking pasta

The secret of cooking pasta is to have a large pan of fast-boiling water with salt or lemon juice added; a small spoonful of oil in the water helps to prevent spills. Ease in long strands of spaghetti, holding them as they bend on contact with the heat. Small pasta shapes should be added a few at a time. Return the water to the boil, half-cover with a tilted lid and cook until only just tender, 6–15 minutes according to type (the packet will tell you). Drain at once in a colander, run cold water through to stop further cooking and drain thoroughly. Toss pasta for salads in a vinaigrette-type dressing while still hot, toss 'accompaniment' pasta in a *little* oil, butter, cream or yoghurt to glisten it, then with chopped herbs or grated Parmesan cheese. Allow 50 g (2 oz) dry pasta as an accompaniment, and 75–100 g (3–4 oz) when it is served as the main dish. Both wholewheat pasta and buckwheat spaghetti, with their nutty flavours, are delicious with a sauce of lightly cooked vegetables – courgettes/zucchini, carrots, leeks, mushrooms, mange-tout peas/Chinese pea pods are all good. Serve pasta steamed with vegetables in a mould (see recipe), in salads, baked with vegetable, fish, meat or cheese sauces, and even with fruit for a hot dessert. To save time, look for wholewheat or spinach lasagne which does not need pre-cooking, and just increase the usual amount of liquid in the sauce by one-quarter (see recipe).

Tuscany lamb

50 g (2 oz) (¼ cup) margarine
500 g (1 lb) lean lamb, trimmed of excess fat, and cut into strips 5 cm × 12 mm (2 × ½ inch)
10 ml (2 teaspoons) wholewheat flour
100 ml (3½ fl oz) (½ cup) hot chicken stock
200 ml (7 fl oz) (⅞ cup) dry cider
175 g (6 oz) (2½ cups) wholewheat wagon-wheel pasta
250-g (8-oz) can artichoke hearts, drained salt and pepper

60 ml (4 tablespoons) (¼ cup) double/heavy cream
15 ml (1 tablespoon) chopped parsley

Melt the margarine and fry the strips of lamb a few at a time for 5 minutes over moderate heat, stirring frequently. Set the lamb aside. Stir the flour into the fat in the pan, pour on the stock, stirring, and bring to the boil. Add the cider and boil, stirring until the sauce thickens. Simmer for 10 minutes.

Meanwhile, cook the pasta in plenty of boiling, salted water for 10–12 minutes,

drain, rinse in cold water and drain again.

Add the lamb and artichoke hearts to the sauce, season with salt and pepper and simmer for 5 minutes. Add the pasta and cream and heat through gently. Garnish with the parsley.

Serves 4

Dried fruit noodles

250 g (8 oz) (¹/₂ lb) wholewheat noodles
salt
90 ml (6 tablespoons) (¹/₃ cup) clear honey
grated rind and juice of 1 lemon
grated rind and juice of 1 orange
125 g (4 oz) (³/₄ cup) dried apricots,
  quartered, soaked and drained
125 g (4 oz) (²/₃ cup) seedless raisins
2 bananas, thinly sliced
25 g (1 oz) (2 tablespoons) butter
50 g (2 oz) (¹/₂ cup) blanched almonds,
  toasted

Cook the noodles in plenty of boiling, salted water for 10 minutes, or until just tender. Drain, rinse and drain. Keep them warm while you make the fruit sauce. Heat the honey, lemon and orange rind and juice, add the apricots and raisins and simmer very gently for 2–3 minutes. Stir in the bananas, just heat through and add the butter. Pour the sauce over the noodles and

garnish with the toasted almonds. Serve at once, with plain yoghurt.

Serves 4

Lasagne verdi with lentil sauce

250 g (8 oz) 'no-pre-cook' lasagne verdi
  SAUCE:
  350 g (12 oz) (1¹/₂ cups) brown lentils,
    soaked and drained
  450 ml (³/₄ pint) (2 cups) water
  30 ml (2 tablespoons) vegetable oil
  25 g (1 oz) (2 tablespoons) margarine
  1 medium onion, finely chopped
  1 medium aubergine/eggplant, finely
    chopped
  125 g (4 oz) (¹/₄ lb) mushrooms,
    chopped
  2 cloves garlic, crushed
  450-g (15-oz) can tomatoes
  60 ml (4 tablespoons) (¹/₄ cup) tomato
    purée
  100 ml (3¹/₂ fl oz) (¹/₂ cup) red wine
  salt and pepper
  a pinch of grated nutmeg
  30 ml (2 tablespoons) chopped parsley
  TOPPING:
  300 ml (¹/₂ pint) (1¹/₄ cups) plain
    yoghurt
  3 eggs
  50 g (2 oz) (¹/₂ cup) Cheddar cheese,
    grated

Cook the lentils in the water for about 1 hour, until they are tender and the water has been absorbed. Heat the oil and margarine and fry the onion, aubergine/eggplant, mushrooms and garlic over low heat for 10 minutes. Add the tomatoes and tomato purée, bring to the boil for 15 minutes. Stir in the lentils and red wine, return to the boil and simmer for 5 minutes. Season with salt, pepper and nutmeg and stir in the parsley.

Cover the base of a greased casserole with sheets of lasagne. Cover with lentil sauce, layers of lasagne and so on, finishing with lentils. Beat together the yoghurt, eggs and cheese and season with salt and pepper. Pour the cheese sauce over. Bake in the oven at 200°C, 400°F, Gas 6 for 50 minutes. Serve hot, with a green salad.

Serves 6

DRINKS

Whether it is a soothing glass of herbal tea at a moment of anxiety, a long glass of chilled fruit-juice cocktail on a hot day or a 'vitality' drink of buttermilk, egg and honey first thing in the morning, drinks of all kinds can do much to affect our well-being and our mood. Herbal infusions, known as tisanes, have soothed nerves and smoothed away minor ailments for centuries and in many parts of the world are taken regularly, as an aid to digestion, after meals. In the Middle East the rigours of the heat are warded off with icy-cold yoghurt drinks, diluted with water and subtly flavoured with herbs, spices or flower-water. The pages that follow are brimming over with healthy, low-calorie ideas for drinks from around the world, all well worth copying. Cheers!

tilleul (lime)   dandelion   comfrey

Tisanes

Herbal teas are made by infusing the fresh or dried leaves, flowers or roots of aromatic plants. A wide variety of the ingredients is available from health-food or speciality shops. The dried materials are sold either loose, as colourful and fragrant as pot-pourri or, convenient for a single serving, in perforated packets, like tea-bags. Many tisanes have almost legendary curative and restorative powers – camomile tea was used for gargling, comfrey for chest complaints, dandelion for liver complaints and as a blood purifier, lime flowers to induce sleep, mint for headaches, nettle as a general tonic, sage for winter ailments and thyme for sinus troubles. Be that as it may, tisanes are both refreshing and comforting and – a positive plus – contain no tannin or caffeine.

For each serving, allow 15 ml (1 tablespoon) fresh herb leaves or 5 ml (1 teaspoon) dried leaves. Lightly crush herb or spice seeds – fennel or caraway – and allow 5 ml (1 teaspoon) per cup. Pour on boiling water, stir, cover and infuse for 5–6 minutes. Strain and serve with a slice of lemon and, if wished, honey to sweeten.

borage   mint   camomile

Fruit and vegetable juices

Health-food shops usually stock a wide range of appetizing natural fruit and vegetable juices – citrus, blackcurrant, pineapple, red and white grape, apple (cloudy is beautiful where apple juice is concerned), tomato, carrot and so on. These are all good as a basis for mixing and matching flavours, blending with fresh fruits and vegetables and prettying-up with decorative garnishes. Check that the products you buy *are* natural and do not contain added sweetening, colouring or flavourings. If you have a liquidizer you can whizz up a zingy harvest of your own. Chop raw vegetables, especially root ones, fairly small and blend them with a little liquid and other flavours. Beetroot is good with lemon juice and green peppers; carrot with orange juice and watercress or parsley; Jerusalem artichokes with apple juice, celery (which always needs straining) and broad-leaved parsley; parsnip with orange juice and honey. Try liquidizing cauliflower with apple juice, onion and a few nuts; fennel with pineapple juice and celery leaves; lettuce with pineapple juice, parsley and onion. The permutations are endless.

Orange barley water

75 g (3 oz) (1/3 cup) pearl barley
thinly pared rind and strained juice of 4 oranges
40 g (1½ oz) (3 tablespoons) light muscovado/brown sugar
ice cubes to serve
orange slices to decorate

Cover the pearl barley with water, bring to the boil and simmer for 3 minutes. Drain and discard the liquid. Rinse the barley and return to the pan with 1.5 litres (2¾ pints) (7 cups) water. Add the orange rind. Bring to the boil, cover and simmer gently for 1½ hours. Strain into a jug and discard the barley and orange rind. Stir in the sugar and the orange juice. Cool and serve chilled, poured over ice cubes. Decorate each glass with orange slices.

Serves 4

Note *Lemon barley water can be made in a similar way, using 4 large lemons.*

Love-apple pick-me-up

2 bunches watercress, trimmed
600 ml (1 pint) (2½ cups) tomato juice, chilled
120 ml (8 tablespoons) (½ cup) vodka
300 ml (½ pint) (1¼ cups) soda water
salt and pepper
ice cubes to serve

Reserving some of the best sprigs for decoration, liquidize the watercress sprigs with a little of the tomato juice. Mix together the remaining juice and the vodka and just before serving top up with the soda water. Season to taste with salt and pepper. Decorate each glass with watercress.

Serves 4

Purple sunset

600 ml (1 pint) (2½ cups) unsweetened
  blackcurrant juice, chilled
60 ml (4 tablespoons) (¼ cup) crème de
  Cassis
juice of 1 orange
450 ml (¾ pint) (2 cups) sparkling
  mineral water, chilled
8 small scoops blackcurrant sorbet
8 small sprigs lemon balm to decorate

Mix together the blackcurrant juice, Cassis
and orange juice. Stir in the mineral water
just before serving. Decorate each glass with
tiny scoops of sorbet and the herb sprigs.

Serves 4

Peach nectar

4 ripe peaches, halved, stoned and peeled
juice of 1 orange
5 ml (1 teaspoon) lemon juice
300 ml (½ pint) (1¼ cups) sparkling rosé
  wine, chilled
a selection of fresh fruits, such as
  strawberries, apple slices, cherries, to
  decorate

Liquidize the peaches with the orange and
lemon juice. Just before serving mix in the
rosé wine. Serve chilled. Decorate each glass
with a mini-'kebab' of fresh fruits. Toss any
sliced fruits that will discolour – apples,
pears, peaches – in lemon juice.

Serves 4

Vitality drinks

Yoghurt, buttermilk, skimmed milk and – for vegetarians, particularly – soya milk make a sound basis for healthy drinks. Blend them with eggs, fruit and vegetables, unsweetened juices, herbs, nuts, wheatgerm and natural flavourings and serve them literally from dawn to dusk. On page 80 you will find other ideas for natural juices you can make in a liquidizer in moments. Try mixing spinach, apple and orange; carrot, watercress and green pepper; celery, pear and hazelnut; grapefruit, parsley and banana, all whizzed up with yoghurt or buttermilk and you will find them surprisingly, revitalizingly good.

Liquid gold

300 ml (½ pint) (1¼ cups) carrot juice,
*   chilled*
300 ml (½ pint) (1¼ cups) buttermilk,
*   chilled*
grated rind and juice of 1 orange
30 ml (2 tablespoons) lemon juice
2 eggs, separated

Blend together the carrot juice, buttermilk, orange and lemon juice and egg yolks and pour into glasses. Whisk the egg whites until frothy, pile on top of the drinks and sprinkle on the orange juice. Serve with straws.

Serves 4

Orchard blossom

2 dessert apples, peeled, cored and
*   chopped*
300 ml (½ pint) (1¼ cups) plain yoghurt,
*   chilled*
300 ml (½ pint) (1¼ cups) cloudy,
*   unsweetened apple juice, chilled*
30 ml (2 tablespoons) clear honey
1 dessert apple, cored and thinly sliced

Liquidize the chopped apple, yoghurt, apple juice and honey. Thread the apple slices on cocktail sticks and decorate each glass.

Serves 4

Rose petal wonder

450 ml (¾ pint) (2 cups) plain yoghurt, chilled
450 ml (¾ pint) (2 cups) skimmed milk, chilled
30 ml (2 tablespoons) lemon juice
2.5 ml (½ teaspoon) triple-strength rosewater
30 ml (2 tablespoons) clear honey, or to taste
rose petals to decorate (optional)

Blend all the ingredients together. Serve well chilled, decorated with rose petals if available. Or with pink Japanese paper umbrellas. This is a version of *lussi*, an Indian drink.

Serves 4

Banana magic

600 ml (1 pint) (2½ cups) plain yoghurt
2 eggs
2 small bananas, sliced
45 ml (3 tablespoons) clear honey
ground cinnamon

Liquidize the yoghurt, eggs, bananas and honey. Decorate each glass with a pinch of cinnamon. Serve at room temperature. This is specially good at breakfast-time.

Serves 4

Apricot ice shaker

175 g (6 oz) (1 cup) dried apricots, soaked
300 ml (½ pint) (1¼ cups) plain yoghurt, chilled
1 can frozen concentrated orange juice
30 ml (2 tablespoons) soured cream
10 ml (2 teaspoons) wheatgerm
4 thin slices orange to decorate

Liquidize the apricots, 300 ml (½ pint) (1¼ cups) of the water in which they were soaked, the yoghurt and orange juice. Pour into glasses, swirl the soured cream on top, sprinkle with wheatgerm and decorate each glass with a slice of orange.

Serves 4

DAIRY FOODS

With dairy produce, it is important to balance the pros, the protein content of animal foods, with the cons – the high fat and cholesterol element. Substituting skimmed milk for the higher-fat types, using low-fat yoghurt with or in place of cream, and yoghurt cheese or cottage cheese sometimes in preference to full-fat kinds are steps in the right direction. Making your own yoghurt and yoghurt cheese in the traditional way is as satisfying and therapeutic as baking wholemeal bread – and even simpler.

Yoghurt

You can use any type of milk for making yoghurt – the lower the fat content of the milk, the fewer calories in the yoghurt. Put 15 ml (1 tablespoon) plain commercial yoghurt or a packet of Bulgarian yoghurt culture into a bowl. Bring 1 litre (1¾ pints) (4½ cups) milk to the boil and leave it to cool to between 47°C (116°F) and 32°C (90°F) – dip in a finger, count to ten and the milk will feel uncomfortably hot. Pour the milk on to the yoghurt, stir well, cover, wrap in a towel and leave undisturbed in a warm place for 6–8 hours. Transfer to the refrigerator and you can store it for up to 1 week. After the first batch, use a little of your own yoghurt as the next 'starter'.

There are various kinds of electrical yoghurt-makers, some thermostatically controlled, which do the job very efficiently.

Stabilizing yoghurt

Yoghurt tends to separate into curds and whey when it is boiled, spoiling the appearance but not the flavour of a cooked dish. To stabilize it, stir 10 ml (2 teaspoons) flour with a little water to make a paste, then stir it gradually into the yoghurt and heat gently, stirring constantly. Simmer for 10 minutes. You can use it at once, or cool it, cover and store it in the refrigerator for up to two weeks. Do not use stabilized yoghurt as a starter.

Yoghurt cheese

To make curd cheese, line a colander with scalded muslin and stand it over a bowl. Pour in the yoghurt, cover and leave for 5–6 hours to drain. Mix the curds with a little salt and chopped fresh herbs or spices – paprika or coriander. Use the whey in soups, casseroles and sauces. Store in the refrigerator in a covered container.

1 litre (1¾ pints) (4½ cups) yoghurt makes about 500 g (1 lb) cheese

Breakfast

There is a refreshingly new look to breakfast nowadays – and a healthy one, too. Low-fat plain yoghurt, light and easy to digest, comes into its own first thing in the morning. For variety, mix yoghurt with orange, pineapple or apple juice; liquidize it with fresh fruits – peaches, apricots, strawberries, stoned cherries – or with any of the dried orchard fruits to serve with muesli and other cereals or, well chilled, as a wake-you-up drink. Whizz in an egg for extra protein, bran or chopped nuts for fibre. Serve yoghurt cheese or cottage cheese on crispbread with slices of fresh fruit or chopped dates and grated apple; make wholewheat sandwiches with yoghurt cheese and thick fruit purée – apricot is specially good; serve cottage cheese mixed with muesli on top of fresh or dried fruit salad; scan the fruit and vegetable juices and the vitality drinks on pages 80–83.

Yoghurt dawn

600 ml (1 pint) (2½ cups) plain yoghurt,
*   chilled*
45 ml (3 tablespoons) wheatgerm
2 small bananas, sliced
60 ml (4 tablespoons) (¼ cup) ground
*   macadamia nuts*
60 ml (4 tablespoons) (¼ cup) chopped
*   macadamia nuts, toasted*

Liquidize the yoghurt, wheatgerm, bananas and ground nuts. Top each glass with toasted nuts. Serve chilled. This early-morning drink is also good poured over muesli.

Serves 4

Almond comfort

600 ml (1 pint) (2½ cups) plain yoghurt, chilled
120 ml (8 tablespoons) (½ cup) double/ heavy cream
30 ml (2 tablespoons) molasses, or black treacle
60 ml (4 tablespoons) (¼ cup) ground almonds
30 ml (2 tablespoons) wheatgerm, plus extra for topping

Blend together the yoghurt, half the cream, molasses or treacle, almonds and wheatgerm. Top each glass with a spoon of cream and sprinkle with wheatgerm.

Serves 4

Fresh-fruit muesli

90 ml (6 tablespoons) (⅓ cup) rolled oat flakes
30 ml (2 tablespoons) wheatgerm
30 ml (2 tablespoons) millet seeds
30 ml (2 tablespoons) pumpkin seeds
30 ml (2 tablespoons) sunflower seeds
30 ml (2 tablespoons) hazelnuts
25 g (1 oz) (¼ cup) candied peel, chopped
2 dessert apples, cored and grated or thinly sliced
3 bananas, thinly sliced
30 ml (2 tablespoons) lemon juice
100 g (4 oz) (¾ cup) fresh or frozen soft fruits, e.g. raspberries, blackberries
fruit juice to serve

Mix together the oat flakes, wheatgerm, seeds, nuts and peel (this mixture can be made up in advance). Toss the apple and banana in lemon juice and stir all the fruit into the muesli. Serve with chilled un-sweetened orange or pineapple juice and orange yoghurt (see next recipe).

Serves 6–8

Orange yoghurt

30 ml (2 tablespoons) clear honey
grated rind and juice of 1 orange
600 ml (1 pint) (2½ cups) plain yoghurt, chilled
3 oranges, segmented

Mix together the honey, orange rind and orange juice. When the honey has dissolved, stir in the yoghurt and the orange segments. Serve chilled.

Serves 6–8

Soup and salad lunches

Snack meals of the soup-and-salad kind are all the more nutritious and enjoyable when dairy foods are high on the ingredient lists. Cool, smooth yoghurt makes a good, contrasting topping (in colour, too) for country soups like borscht, and mushroom, tomato and watercress. Stir miniature raw vegetable sticks into a half-and-half mixture of chilled yoghurt and tomato juice. Use buttermilk to make both cauliflower and ground almond soups, and for special occasions blend it with a pinch of cinnamon and fruit purée – raspberry, rhubarb, blackberry or cherry – for first courses that get talked about. Yoghurt cheese can be tossed with nuts and rolled into bite-sized balls; mixed with chopped pineapple and sliced black olives; added to finely diced carrot, raisins and caraway seeds; mixed with prawns and chopped green pepper – this slightly sour, tangy home-made cheese goes well with green salads (spinach, endive, chicory, watercress). Snack meals are nutritionally much more than snacks.

Borscht

*500 g (1 lb) raw beetroot, peeled and
    shredded*
1 large onion, finely chopped
*250 g (8 oz) (2¼ cups) firm white
    cabbage, shredded*
grated rind and juice of 1 orange
1 bouquet garni
30 ml (2 tablespoons) tomato purée
*1 litre (1¾ pints) (4½ cups) hot chicken
    or beef stock*
30 ml (2 tablespoons) red wine vinegar
salt and pepper
30 ml (2 tablespoons) sultanas
200 ml (7 fl oz) (1 cup) plain yoghurt
sunflower seeds to serve

Put the beetroot, onion and cabbage into a pan with the orange rind and juice and bouquet garni. Mix together the tomato purée, stock and vinegar and pour over. Season with salt and pepper. Bring to the boil and simmer over low heat for 50 minutes, until all the vegetables are tender. Stir in the sultanas. Swirl the yoghurt on top and serve with the sunflower seeds.

Serves 6–8

Yoghurt cheese and walnut worlds

250 g (8 oz) (1 cup) yoghurt cheese
   (page 85), chilled
30 ml (2 tablespoons) plain yoghurt
10 ml (2 teaspoons) chopped marjoram, or
   parsley
100 g (4 oz) (1 cup) walnuts, finely
   chopped
salt and pepper

Beat together the cheese and yoghurt and beat in the herbs and half the chopped walnuts. Season with salt and pepper and chill. Shape into balls the size of walnuts. Roll them in the remaining chopped nuts.

Makes about 30

Note You can serve the cheese balls, speared with cocktail sticks, as an appetizer: they look specially good arranged on vine leaves. For an interesting salad dish thread them on kebab sticks or fine skewers with sliced mushrooms, avocado, tomato wedges and cucumber dice (toss the vegetables in a lemon dressing first).

Dairy salad

125 g (4 oz) (¼ lb) young spinach leaves
2 heads chicory
1 small pineapple, skinned, cored and cut
   into rings
250 g (8 oz) (1 cup) yoghurt cheese
   (page 85)
75 g (3 oz) (½ cup) feta or Wensleydale
   cheese, crumbled
2 hard-boiled eggs, sliced
   DRESSING:
   60 ml (4 tablespoons) (¼ cup) salad oil
   45 ml (3 tablespoons) pineapple juice
   5 ml (1 teaspoon) cider vinegar
   salt and pepper

Mix together the dressing ingredients. Wash, trim and dry the salad leaves. Tear any large ones and toss them together. Arrange on a serving dish with the pineapple rings around the edge. Mix together the cheeses and pile in the centre. Garnish with the egg slices. Serve the dressing separately. This salad is a meal in itself, with plenty of wholewheat bread. It is also good served with cold chicken.

Serves 4–6

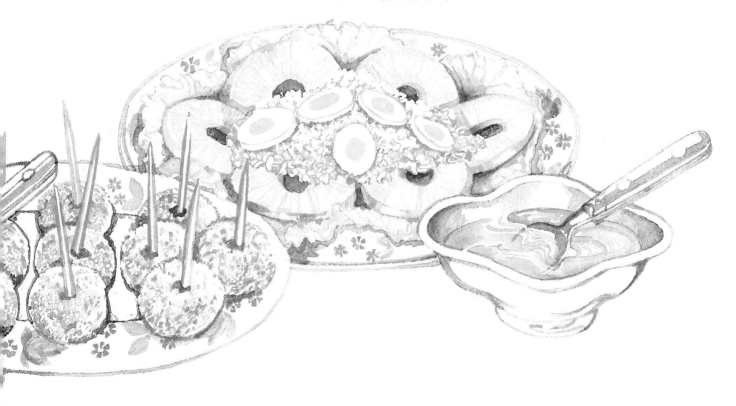

Main dishes

Tandoori chicken in a flame-red and fiery sauce served with palate-cooling cucumber salad – two recipes which demonstrate the incredible main-meal versatility of yoghurt. Follow the 'tandoori' method to cook leg of lamb in a turmeric and ginger sauce; spare rib of pork with tomato purée and paprika, and poussins (baby chickens) with tarragon and whole-grain mustard. Simmer cabbage-leaf parcels of meat, rice and herbs, or lamb and lemon meat-balls, in yoghurt in the Turkish way. Bake white fish in yoghurt with mint and the 'sweet' spices – cardamom, coriander and cumin – and poach fillets with crushed fennel seed and the frondy, aromatic leaves. Make a quick and delicious baked topping by beating eggs and grated cheese into yoghurt – it is good on lasagne (page 77), casserole of courgettes/zucchini and tomatoes, and on potato slices layered with onions; it also makes a fantastic quiche filling. Toss cooked vegetables with yoghurt – lower in fat than butter – and have it on hand to rescue an over-spiced or salty sauce or to use as an instant, always interesting garnish.

Tandoori chicken

4 chicken pieces, skinned
5 ml (1 teaspoon) ground turmeric
5 ml (1 teaspoon) ground ginger
5 ml (1 teaspoon) ground cumin
2.5 ml (½ teaspoon) chilli powder
2.5 ml (½ teaspoon) ground fenugreek
5 ml (1 teaspoon) salt
2 cloves garlic, crushed
2 bay leaves, crumbled
15 ml (1 tablespoon) tomato purée
30 ml (2 tablespoons) lemon juice
450 ml (¾ pint) (2 cups) plain yoghurt
100 g (4 oz) (½ cup) ghee (clarified butter)
paprika pepper
1 lemon, quartered, to garnish

Prick the chicken flesh all over with a sterilized darning needle. Mix together the turmeric, ginger, cumin, chilli, fenugreek and salt. Stir the garlic, bay leaves, tomato purée and lemon juice into the yoghurt and stir in the spices. Line a casserole with foil. Pour in half the ghee, add the chicken and pour over the yoghurt mixture. Cover tightly with foil and with the lid.

Cook in the oven at 190° C, 375° F, Gas 5 for 1 hour. Remove the top piece of foil. Rub paprika into the chicken to cover it completely. Cook, uncovered, for a further 20 minutes. Pour off the yoghurt sauce and serve it separately. Garnish the chicken with lemon wedges.

Serve with brown rice and chapattis.

Serves 4

Yoghurt salad (tzajiki)

600 ml (1 pint) (2½ cups) plain yoghurt,
*   chilled*
2.5 ml (½ teaspoon) salt
2 cloves garlic, crushed
1 small cucumber, peeled, seeded and
*   finely diced*
30 ml (2 tablespoons) chopped mint
chilli powder to garnish

Stir together the yoghurt, salt, garlic,
cucumber and mint, cover and chill for 30
minutes. Taste and adjust seasoning.
Garnish with a sprinkling of chilli. Serve
with spiced dishes – curried meat, fish,
vegetables and chilli beans.

__Note__ To vary this Balkan salad, stir in 25 g (1 oz)
(⅓ cup) desiccated coconut for an Indian flavour;
or replace the cucumber and mint with 2 finely
chopped green peppers and chopped parsley; or
with 2 medium grated carrots and 45 ml (3
tablespoons) chopped mango chutney; or with 2
mashed bananas and 15 ml (1 tablespoon)
chopped coriander leaves.

Desserts

Rich and creamy puddings are so often the downfall of people trying to limit their daily intake of animal fats and count the calories. If total prohibition seems unacceptably drastic, let the maxim be 'just a little' – and then only on highdays and holidays. Blend plain yoghurt half-and-half with cream for traditional favourites such as crème brûlée (see recipe for fig brûlée), zabaglione and lemon posset. Make fruity ice creams with milk and yoghurt (see example on page 25) and no one would know you have not used cream. Top fruit salads with low-fat yoghurt cheese or cottage cheese instead of pouring cream. Use skimmed milk for baked puddings – such as rice – and as it is so bland be rather more heavy-handed with the flavourings. And when you *do* serve cream – such as our home-made *crème fraîche* – be mean and use it only as a garnish. You have to be cruel to be kind.

Fig brûlée

4 egg yolks
75 g (3 oz) (¹/₃ cup) light muscovado/
* brown sugar*
300 ml (½ pint) (1¹/₄ cups) double/heavy
* cream*
300 ml (½ pint) (1¹/₄ cups) plain yoghurt
2 scented geranium leaves
6 fresh figs, sliced

Beat the egg yolks with 25 g (1 oz) (2 tablespoons) of the sugar. Heat the cream, yoghurt and geranium leaves in the top of a double boiler, or a bowl fitted over a pan with simmering water. When the mixture is just below boiling point, remove it from the heat. Pour a little into the egg mixture, beat well and add it back to the cream. Cook over low heat, stirring constantly, until the custard thickens. Discard the leaves.

Slice the figs and arrange them in the base of a flame-proof dish. Pour on the cream mixture through a strainer. Sprinkle the remaining sugar on top and caramellize under a hot grill. Leave to cool, then chill. Crack the caramel with a spoon before serving.

Serves 6

Apricot sorbet

1 orange
250 g (8 oz) (1½ cups) dried apricots,
  soaked (reserve the liquid)
250 g (8 oz) (1 cup) light muscovado/
  brown sugar
2 egg whites
scented geranium leaves to decorate

Thinly pare the rind from the orange and squeeze the juice. Cook the apricots with 300 ml (½ pint) (1¼ cups) of the soaking water, the orange rind and juice and sugar for 20 minutes. Remove the orange rind and liquidize the fruit. Cool and then chill. Pour into a container, cover and freeze for 1 hour until the mixture is frozen on the outside and mushy inside. Whisk very thoroughly to break down the ice crystals, cover and freeze for 2 hours. Stiffly beat the egg whites and fold them in. Cover and freeze again until firm. Leave to mellow in the main part of the refrigerator for 30 minutes before serving.

Serve in scoops, decorated with scented geranium leaves.

Serves 6

Note *This is a lively way to use left-over egg whites. Other fruit sorbets can be made in a similar way: use blackcurrant or blackberry purée flavoured with Cassis, gooseberry with elderflowers or scented geranium leaves, strawberry with rosewater.*

Crème fraîche

30 ml (2 tablespoons) buttermilk
300 ml (½ pint) (1¼ cups) double/heavy
  cream

Stir the buttermilk into the cream. Cover and leave at room temperature for 24 hours. The resulting slightly sour-tasting cream, perfect with soft summer fruits, will keep well in the refrigerator to 8–10 days.

Makes 300 ml (½ pint) (1¼ cups)

VEGETABLE PRODUCTS

Nutritionally, the most important vegetable product is beancurd, or *tofu*, which is made from soya beans. The curd is high in polyunsaturated fats, has no cholesterol and is an important source of protein among vegetarians (and non-vegetarians) in China and Japan. To make it the beans are cooked, mashed, sieved and pressed into moist, milky-white blocks which are virtually tasteless and have the consistency of thick blancmange. There are three main types: the plain *tofu*, one which is lightly grilled, and one which is deep-fried to a golden brown. All are available in cans. Plain *tofu* also comes in two-portion-size cartons. Beancurd can be served as part of a salad, stir-fried with vegetables, in soups and in fish and meat dishes (see *sukiyaki* recipe, page 97). Bean paste (*miso*) is available in both sweet and salted forms and is used in dishes as varied as fish soup and cakes. The various types of dried seaweed offer exciting new culinary experiences, as melt-in-the mouth appetizers and vegetable accompaniments. And dried mushrooms present a flavour range impossible to achieve with the fresh varieties of fungus available in Western stores. The selection below starts with the Chinese-inspired recipes.

Steamed dumplings

250 g (8 oz) filo or strudel pastry sheets
soy sauce to serve
   PORK FILLING:
   250 g (8 oz) (1 cup) lean pork,
     finely minced
   2 spring/green onions, finely
     chopped
   1 clove garlic, crushed
   4–6 young spinach leaves,
     shredded
   2.5 ml (½ teaspoon) sugar
   10 ml (2 teaspoons) soy sauce
   5 ml (1 teaspoon) sesame oil
CHICKEN FILLING:
   250 g (8 oz) (1 cup) chicken meat,
     finely minced
   2 small leeks, finely chopped
   2 spring/green onions, finely
     chopped
   1 clove garlic, crushed
   15 ml (1 tablespoon) soy sauce
   5 ml (1 teaspoon) sugar
   10 ml (2 teaspoons) sesame oil

Mix together each filling, working the mixtures to a moist paste. Cover and set aside for at least 1 hour.

Cut the pastry into 7.5-cm (3-inch) squares. Divide the fillings between them, spooning a small mound of filling into the centre. Fold over the sides to make neat 'envelopes' and tuck in the sides, allowing room for expansion. Steam over fast-boiling water for 10 minutes. Serve hot, with soy sauce.

Serves 6

Stir-fried mushrooms and legumes

8 dried Chinese mushrooms
45 ml (3 tablespoons) peanut oil
2 spring/green onions, thinly sliced
2 thin slices fresh root ginger, chopped
2 garlic cloves, crushed
250 g (8 oz) (½ lb) mange-tout peas/
  Chinese pea pods, topped and tailed
250 g (8 oz) (½ lb) fresh bean
  sprouts, washed and drained
20 ml (4 teaspoons) soya sauce
30 ml (2 tablespoons) chicken stock
15 g (½ oz) (1 tablespoon) lard
100 g (4 oz) (1 cup) cashews

Soak the mushrooms in water for 30 minutes. Drain, pat dry and slice. Heat the oil in a wok or heavy frying-pan and stir-fry the onions, ginger and garlic over high heat for 1 minute. Add the mushrooms, pea pods and bean sprouts and stir-fry for 1½ minutes. Pour on the sauce and stock, stir well, lower the heat and simmer for 2–3 minutes, until the liquid has evaporated. Add the lard in small pieces and stir to glaze the vegetables. Stir in the cashews. Serve at once, with rice.

Serves 4

Seaweed salad

50 g (2 oz) dried kelp seaweed
30 ml (2 tablespoons) sesame oil
2 cloves garlic, crushed
1 fresh or dried red chilli, thinly sliced
2 thin slices fresh root ginger, finely
  chopped
  SAUCE:
  10 ml (2 teaspoons) soy sauce
  10 ml (2 teaspoons) red wine vinegar
  5 ml (1 teaspoon) white distilled
    vinegar
  salt and pepper
  a pinch of monosodium glutamate
  5 ml (1 teaspoon) sugar

Boil the seaweed for 10 minutes, then rinse it thoroughly under cold, running water to clean it. Drain and pat dry. Cut into matchstick strips.

Heat the oil in a wok or frying-pan and stir-fry the garlic, chilli and ginger over moderate heat for 1 minute. Add the seaweed and sauce, quickly stir-fry to mix. Serve cold as an appetizer or salad accompaniment.

Serves 4

Japanese dishes

Many health-food shops, besides specialized Oriental grocers, sell the dried vegetables, seasonings and flavourings that characterize Chinese (on the preceding two pages) and Japanese cuisine. These recipes feature bean curd, bean paste, dried mushrooms, kelp seaweed, bamboo shoots and *shirataki* noodles, made from a vegetable root. All the dishes are quick to cook. The secret lies in the careful preparation – each piece of meat or vegetable cut to exactly the same size – and the presentation. Decorate the table for a Japanese meal simply. White chrysanthemum flower-heads floating in a bowl of water are a perfect foil for the food.

Matsutake gohan (rice with mushrooms)

250 g (8 oz) (1 cup) long-grain white rice
175 g (6 oz) dried mushrooms
600 ml (1 pint) (2½ cups) water
a piece of kelp seaweed to flavour
  (optional)
30 ml (2 tablespoons) soy sauce
30 ml (2 tablespoons) sake
salt

Wash and drain the rice. Wash the mushrooms, soak them in water for 30 minutes, then drain and cut them into thin strips. Put the rice, water, kelp if used, soy sauce and *sake* into a pan, bring to the boil and discard the kelp. Add the mushrooms and salt, bring to the boil, cover and simmer for 15–20 minutes, until the rice is tender and the water has been absorbed. Set aside in a warm place for 5 minutes before serving.

Serves 4

Sukiyaki

750 g (1½ lb) rump steak, or topside
250 g (12 oz) (¾ lb) beancurd, drained
    and dried
25 g (1 oz) (2 tablespoons) suet, or lard
8 spring/green onions, sliced into 5-cm
    (2-inch) pieces
1 medium onion, thinly sliced into rings
100-g (4-oz) can bamboo shoots, drained
    and thinly sliced
150-g (5-oz) can shirataki noodles,
    drained
350 g (12 oz) (¾ lb) flat fresh mushrooms
350 g (12 oz) (¾ lb) young spinach
    leaves, trimmed
6 eggs
    SAUCE:
    75 ml (5 tablespoons) (⅓ cup) soy
      sauce
    60 ml (4 tablespoons) (¼ cup) sake, or
      dry sherry
    30 ml (2 tablespoons) sugar
    75 ml (5 tablespoons) (⅓ cup) dashi, or
      chicken stock

Ask the butcher to slice the meat paper-thin on a bacon slicer. To do so yourself, partly freeze it to stiffen it, place the meat on a board with one hand flat on top, and carve it horizontally with a very sharp knife. Cut it into 7.5-cm (3-inch) squares. Toast the beancurd on both sides in a dry, non-stick frying-pan over moderate heat for 3–4 minutes on each side. Mix together the sauce ingredients.

In true Japanese style, before starting to cook arrange the main ingredients for the dish on a plate. *Sukiyaki* is usually cooked at the table, each diner taking a little from the pan as it is ready and dipping it into a beaten egg in his serving bowl.

Grease a heavy pan with suet or lard over moderate heat. Cook a portion of the meat and onions for 2 minutes, stirring constantly. Add a proportion of the beancurd, bamboo shoots, noodles, mushrooms and spinach and sprinkle with some of the sauce. Stir-fry until the spinach has collapsed and the other vegetables are cooked. Serve at once with plain boiled rice. Continue cooking the remaining ingredients in the same way.

Serves 6

Stuffed mushrooms

24 dried mushrooms
225 ml (8 fl oz) (1 cup) dashi, or chicken
    stock
30 ml (2 tablespoons) soy sauce
30 ml (2 tablespoons) sugar
250 g (8 oz) (½ lb) cooked, shelled fresh
    or frozen shrimps
1 small egg white
salt
a pinch of monosodium glutamate
7.5 ml (1½ teaspoons) cornflour/
    cornstarch

Soak the mushrooms in water for 30 minutes, drain, cut off the stems and pat them dry. Bring the stock, soy sauce and sugar to the boil, add the mushrooms and simmer for 10–12 minutes. Drain and dry the mushrooms.

Grind the shrimps to a paste in a blender and mix with the egg white, salt, monosodium glutamate and cornflour/cornstarch. Spoon the paste into the mushroom caps. Steam over boiling stock or water for 10 minutes to set the paste. Serve hot or cold, as appetizers. A good accompaniment is sliced *daikon*, Japanese pickled radish.

Makes 24 mushrooms

FLAVOURINGS

For many of us, the most exciting shelves in the health-food shops are those displaying bottles, cans, cartons, boxes, packets and bags of flavourings: the most exciting, yet often the most unfathomable, since so many are sold with neither translation nor cooking instructions.

However unfamiliar they may seem, it is well worth seeking closer acquaintance with these ingredients, for they do not only bring variety to the comparatively limited number of basic foods; at very little cost they offer an enthusiastic cook the taste of virtually every region in the world. A whole bream, marinated Chinese-style in wine, vinegar and soy sauce, steamed then garnished with dried shrimps, will be quite a different experience from the same fish pickled in brine, dried chillis and mustard seeds – a medieval European preserving method. A tuna fish and cucumber salad dressed with soya-bean paste (*shiro-miso*) will have little in common with a *salade niçoise* – except the basic ingredients.

Soya products

Among the best-known bottled sauce preparations is soy sauce, indispensable in all kinds of Chinese and Japanese cooking. The sauce is manufactured from soya beans which are soaked, mashed and fermented with wheat or barley flour for at least three months. In that time the natural yeasts produce a salty liquid with a very strong and highly concentrated flavour. This sauce is used both as a cooking ingredient and as a table condiment.

Japanese and Chinese soy sauces, though interchangeable, have different characteristic flavours. The colour can range from light to dark brown. Among the Japanese types *tamari*, or *shoyu*, is dark and full of flavour, while *koikuchi* is darker still, with a syrupy consistency. Among Chinese soy sauces, the lightest in both colour and flavour comes from the Canton region; dark soy is richer and more strongly flavoured.

As always, beware of imitations. There are cheap simulated soy sauces based on hydrolized vegetable protein. These preparations are flavoured with salt and deep-coloured with caramel and lack the richness of the natural products.

Soy sauce is an essential ingredient in so many Oriental dishes: sweet and sour sauces; marinades; pastes to toss meat and fish in before stir-frying; with rice wine and spices for stir-braising; in salad dressing; and as a dip on the table, where it is served in tiny individual dishes. Its use need not, however, be limited to Eastern dishes. A dash of soy sauce adds depth of flavour to barbecue sauce, meat soups and casseroles – of beef, hare and venison especially – and to the stock when cooking rice and other grains. As a condiment it is particularly good with rice, fish, chicken and egg dishes.

Another feature of Chinese cuisine which has similar uses is oyster sauce, made from liquidized oysters and soy sauce. It has a strong but not a fishy flavour.

When you want the flavour of soy sauce in a dish that also needs thickening – a sauce or soup, for instance – use *miso*, a Japanese paste made from fermented soya beans. As this is made with the whole beans it also provides protein and dietary fibre. A similar product is *miso* soya purée, made in Japan from soya beans and brown rice. As an example, try *miso* vegetable soup.

Miso vegetable soup

30 ml (2 tablespoons) vegetable oil
1 large onion, sliced
4 stalks celery, thinly sliced
2 medium carrots, diced
1 clove garlic, finely chopped
350 g (12 oz) (3⅓ cups) firm white
  cabbage, shredded
1 litre (1¾ pints) (4½ cups) chicken stock
60 ml (4 tablespoons) (¼ cup) miso soya
  purée
60 ml (4 tablespoons) (¼ cup) cooked
  brown rice
radish slices or sliced spring/green onions
  to garnish

Heat the oil and sauté the onion and celery over moderate heat for 2–3 minutes, stirring once or twice. Add the carrots and garlic, cook for 2 minutes, then pour on the stock. Bring to the boil, cover and simmer for 20 minutes. Add the cabbage, return to the boil, cover and simmer for 10 minutes, until the cabbage is barely tender. Stir in the purée and the rice and re-heat. Garnish with the sliced radishes or onion.

Serves 4

Essences and oils

When it comes to those tiny bottles of headily-scented liquids, health-food shops almost invariably do the selection for you, sorting through the maze of manufactured look-and-smell-alikes, and offering only the pure, natural essences: vanilla extract to add to cakes, biscuits/cookies, custards, milk drinks and all chocolate dishes; grapefruit, orange and lemon oils extracted from the peel of the fruit, for sponge cakes, frostings, ice creams and sorbets; peppermint oil for frostings, fondants and fudge, and flower-waters for Middle Eastern dishes.

Essences are made in two ways: by distillation, whereby the liquid is evaporated and then condensed to concentrate the flavour; and by maceration, whereby the plant material is soaked in a liquid which draws out the flavour. Orange-flower water and rose water are made in this way.

Extracts are concentrated flavourings, usually made with ethyl alcohol. Almond extract is made from bitter almonds; one or two drops intensifies the flavour of ground almonds used in halva, marzipan and cakes. For a more subtle flavour, use sweet almond oil. Vanilla extract should not be confused with vanillin, which is made from oil of cloves.

Natural essences include extracts, essential oils and flower-waters. When artificial ingredients are included the product should be labelled as a 'flavouring', a point worth looking out for in the small print.

These essences are so concentrated that whereas one or two drops can work wonders in a dish, one or two more can ruin it. Measure them out drop by drop the easy way, by dipping in a wooden cocktail stick.

You can achieve a hint of the flavour in baked and sweet dishes by making your own infused sugar. Store a vanilla pod, a sprig of bay leaves or rosemary, the thinly pared rind of an orange or lemon in a jar of light muscovado or demerara sugar – and you will not need the bottles at all.

Herb and spice oils and vinegars

Flavoured vegetable oils and vinegars can easily give you the collecting habit. Each one has a slightly different characteristic to offer, and not only for salad dressings and sauces. Use marjoram oil to make wholewheat spaghetti glisten; toss steamed cabbage in a dash of caraway vinegar; use flavoured oils and vinegars in marinades, especially when you have no fresh herbs.

Health-food shops sell a range of these oils and vinegars, or you can easily make your own. To each 600 ml (1 pint) (2½ cups) vegetable oil or white vinegar, add 60 ml (4 tablespoons) (¼ cup) lightly bruised herb leaves – parsley, marjoram, tarragon, chervil or whatever – or the same measure of toasted and lightly crushed spice seeds – fennel, aniseed, caraway and so on. Cork or cover the bottle, shake it every day and leave to infuse for about three weeks. Strain, pour into fresh bottles and, for herb oils and vinegars, add a fresh sprig of the herb for decoration. These home-made cooking preparations make super gifts.

HERBS AND SPICES

Health-food shops carry an almost bewildering range of dried herbs and spices, both 'loose' and ready-packed in brand-labelled jars. Some also sell fresh herb plants, so that you can grow your own favourites in the garden or on a sunny window-sill.

There is nothing new about cooking with herbs and spices: wild herbs were among man's earliest plant foods, used simply to flavour a stock-pot broth of vegetables and pulses or taken to ward off or alleviate all kinds of ills. For details of soothing herbal drinks, known as tisanes, see page 79. Spices from the Far Eastern tropical regions were so highly valued as flavourings, preservatives and as health foods – to aid digestion, encourage sleep, as diuretics and so on – that battles were fought, by land and sea, and protection rackets proliferated so that extortionate prices could be maintained.

Our own battles today are for healthier ingredients and a greater awareness of which foods are beneficial and which are harmful to health. Here, herbs and spices are as important as they ever were, compensating for the flavour of foods we are trying to cut down on – butter, eggs and cream in sauces, for instance – and adding infinite variety to plain, wholesome fare. A slice of wholemeal bread spread with thyme-flavoured yoghurt cheese; a salad of dried pulses tossed with fresh basil, chervil and summer savory; yoghurt sauce spiked with turmeric, cumin and paprika to elevate chicken; a compote of dried fruits fragrant with the sweet aromatics, allspice, cinnamon or mace – these are today's ways of using herbs and spices.

Buying and storing

Buy dried herbs and spices in very small quantities that you will use within a maximum of six months. Store them in a dry, cool place away from strong light. No matter how attractive and convenient it is to have a rack of clear glass jars on a kitchen wall, a cupboard is kinder to their contents. Sunlight draws out the fragrant oils and soon you are left with contents of nondescript appearance and without any discernible aroma.

Whenever possible buy whole spices and, when you need to, grind or grate them yourself – use a pestle and mortar, or keep a hand grinder for the purpose. Unless you enjoy spices with *everything*, it is not a good idea to use the coffee mill. Whole spices retain more of their characteristics and for longer periods, in addition to which if you buy them whole you can judge the quality, and there will be no risk of adulteration by inferior ingredients.

Using herbs

Dried herbs have a much more concentrated flavour than fresh ones. Use them in roughly half the quantity – less if they are still full of aroma. When 15 ml (1 tablespoon) fresh herbs is called for, substitute 5–7.5 ml (1–1½ teaspoons) dried.

Many recipes suggest using a small bag of herbs, a *bouquet garni*, which can be of fresh or dried leaves. Bay leaves, parsley and thyme usually form the basis of these herb 'pot-pourris', with the addition of basil, marjoram, rosemary, oregano or (especially for fish dishes) tarragon. You can buy ready-made *bouquets* of dried herbs in many health-food shops. Store them in an airtight container away from the light.

To use dried herbs in cold sauces – a basil

and yoghurt dressing to serve with tomato salad, for example – reconstitute them first in boiling water, 5 ml (1 teaspoon) herbs to 10 ml (2 teaspoons) water, then strain them. Herb- and spice-flavoured oils and vinegars make particularly good salad dressings – see page 100 for ideas.

Drying and freezing herbs

If you have the opportunity to grow fresh herbs, take it. There is nothing to compare with the scent of a sprig of fresh mint cooking with mange-tout peas/Chinese pea pods or summer savory with baby broad beans; nothing does as much to lift bulghar salad as a generous sprinkling of chopped mint and parsley, and nothing gives a bowl of spaghetti the flavour of Italy like a sauce heady with fresh basil leaves.

Growing your own herbs means you have the chance to develop a cottage industry too, by drying and freezing some of your harvest. Pick only the young shoots, which contain more natural oils and have more aroma. To dry them, hang them in bunches in a warm, airy place for about a week until the leaves feel papery. Strip them from the stalks, crumble them gently, store in airtight containers and label clearly.

To freeze herbs, pack them on the stem in plastic bags or rigid containers, then strip off the leaves as you need them. Or chop the leaves, pack them in ice-cube trays, fill with water and freeze. Thaw the cubes in a strainer – result, fresh-as-a-daisy chopped herbs.

Using spices

Spices – the dried seeds, berries, bark or root of aromatic plants – are packed pungently full of scent and flavour. Try one or two whole cloves in apple pie or a compote of pears; two or three seeds of aniseed added to the water when steaming cauliflower or carrots; a couple of gratings of nutmeg over 'vitality' drinks and milk puddings; a thread of saffron infused in water to flavour rice and colour it golden, especially in Spanish cooking – a little goes a long way.

In these and many other dishes, infusing whole spices – tied in muslin, if need be, for easy extraction – gives a more subtle, and better distribution of, flavour. For a fuller flavour still, roast or toast spice seeds before use, in the oven, under the grill or in a heavy frying-pan for about 10 minutes. This has the added advantage of making them more brittle, and easier to grind.

When powdered spices are called for – in curries, casseroles, bread, cakes and biscuits/cookies, crumble toppings and so on – be sure to mix them thoroughly with other ingredients. If the spices are stirred with the onion and garlic before the stock is added, or mixed to a paste with a little oil, you will prevent a 'raw' taste in savoury dishes, and sifting them with flour and other dry ingredients is an elementary precaution in baking.

As most spices are grown in the tropics, there are fewer 'grow-your-own' possibilities in temperate climates. Fennel, caraway, coriander, dill, onion, celery and poppy seeds are all potential and worthwhile crops, many of them offering double-value fragrant leaves besides. Cut the stems as soon as the seeds start to dry on the plant, tie paper (not plastic) bags firmly over the seed-heads and hang them upside-down to dry in a warm airy place. Spread the harvested seeds on trays in the airing cupboard or in the sunshine for a couple of days (watching out for even gentle breezes!) and store, clearly labelled, in airtight containers.

FATS AND OILS

One of the most important and complex issues relating to health foods is the one of fats *vs* oils. Many myths and misunderstandings abound, complicated by the fact that medical opinion in the past produced varying conclusions about the merits and demerits of the different types of fat. All very confusing!

There now seems no doubt that a high intake of fat is a key factor in the incidence of coronary heart disease, the greatest single cause of death in the Western world. At present in Britain as much as 42 per cent of body energy is supplied by the fat consumed (with 13 per cent protein and 45 per cent carbohydrates); this is now considered dangerously high. In the findings of a study carried out by the World Health Organization and published in 1982, it was recommended that, to achieve a much more healthy and balanced diet, fat should be only 30 per cent of the total intake. This 'share' should be made up in equal parts by saturated fats (at present comprising 20 per cent of the body's total intake), polyunsaturated fats (now only 5 per cent) and mono-unsaturated fats (currently 17 per cent). The fat in all foods is made up of these three fats in widely differing proportions. It is a matter of juggling with ingredients to achieve a satisfactory balance.

What effect would such a change of emphasis have on the weekly shopping basket? First, it is necessary to have a clear understanding of the terms.

Saturated fats, the 'baddies' where health is concerned, are recognizable as those that set hard at room temperature and are mainly of animal origin. Foods with a high level of saturated fats include butter, lard, dripping, suet, hard margarines and the fat on meat – the visible rim around a pork chop and the hidden marbling in a piece of steak. They are also present in significant amounts in dairy products such as whole milk, full-fat cheeses and cream and in some vegetable products. Coconuts have a particularly high content.

It is these saturated fatty acids which contribute to the increase in the amount of cholesterol – a waxy, fat-like substance – in the bloodstream, which can develop into a blockage of the arteries.

Polyunsaturated fats are present to a small degree in meats and to a greater extent as the oil in fish. They are liquid or very soft at room temperature and familiar in the form of vegetable oils for cooking and salads. Soya-bean oil, corn oil, sunflower and safflower oils are all high in polyunsaturates. So are some soft margarines and white vegetable fats – but not all, so check the labels.

A great deal of controversy has raged over claims that polyunsaturates actually lower cholesterol levels in the blood. What is clear is that to implement the WHO recommendations it would be necessary to double the intake of those fats at the expense of saturated and mono-unsaturated fats.

Mono-unsaturated fats are thought to be neutral in the incidence of heart disease. They, too, are liquid at room temperature; olive oil is an example.

Unrefined and refined oils

After the battle between saturated and unsaturated fats, there is the question of unrefined (natural) and refined oils. This is a straightforward matter of the extraction process used, and in no way indicates the proportion of poly- or mono-unsaturates in the oil.

Health-food advocates will prefer oils processed by the traditional cold-pressing or expeller-pressing methods, which produce a slightly cloudy oil with its natural colour, the flavour of the plant seed, some seed particles and juice. Because of their superior flavour, unrefined oils such as olive, sesame, safflower, peanut (also known as groundnut or arachide), wheatgerm, walnut and corn oils are in any case most suitable for salad dressings and dishes in which the character of the oil is important – hummus, for example. The disadvantage is that unrefined oils have a short shelf life – no more than six months.

Refined oils will keep for up to a year without deteriorating. These are produced by a much more economic process in which solvents are used to extract the maximum oil from the seed. Refined sunflower and soya-bean oils, for example, are useful for deep frying.

Margarine

Most margarines are made from vegetable oils, milk, salt and colourings and some contain animal fats, fish oil or butter as well. For hard margarines, which have the consistency of butter, the fats are hardened by having hydrogen passed through them, and are therefore 'saturated' fats. Most soft margarines, the ones which are sold in tubs and remain soft under refrigeration, contain a high proportion of polyunsaturated fats, and are therefore better for health. All of these margarines have the same calorific value as butter – about 730 calories per 100 g (4 oz) (½ cup). Low-fat spread is made by mixing hard-saturated margarine with water.

Flashpoints

Oils have a higher flashpoint – the temperature at which they will flare – than butter. For this reason, oil and butter are often mixed half and half to give a combination of the dairy flavour and a higher frying temperature.

Most oils will smoke at 230 °C, 450 °F, and reach flashpoint at 325 °C, 617 °F. Olive oil has much lower levels, smoking at 170 °C, 325 °F, and reaching flashpoint at 285 °C, 545 °F.

Oil for frying should be heated slowly. Both rapid heating and overheating cause deterioration. For deep frying the recom-mended temperature range is 170 °–200 °C, 325 °–400 °F. If food is cooked at too high a temperature it will burn on the outside before being cooked through, and at too low a temperature it will absorb the oil – with unappetizing and unhealthy results.

Characteristics

For the characteristics and uses of each type of oil, please turn to the glossary.

SWEETENERS

It seems that the controversy between the properties of honey and sugar as a source of energy and sweetness is not a new one. In 300 BC one of Alexander the Great's generals referred to the sugar cane as 'a reed that produced honey without the aid of bees'. Sugar-making was known in India as long ago as 3000 BC, but until the seventeenth century honey was the only form of sweetener commonly used in Europe.

Sugar

Sugar is produced from both sugar cane and sugar beet. The cane is a perennial plant which grows in tropical regions to a height of 6.5 m (21 feet). It was first cultivated in the Far East, Asia and the Mediterranean countries. Columbus took the cane to the Caribbean where it grew so well that the centre of the trade shifted to the West Indies.

In the eighteenth century a German chemist discovered that sugar could also be extracted and refined from beet, a crop which can be grown in temperate climates. It is now cultivated and processed in the UK, the west coast of the USA, France, West Germany, Poland and the USSR.

All sugars are high in calories – many dieticians evocatively term them 'empty' calories – but natural, unrefined sugars extracted from sugar cane do contain valuable minerals and trace elements. Many of these are processed out and lost in the refining of white and artificially browned sugars. And so in the case of sugar, as with rice and flour, it may be said that we pay a high price in health terms for the white, refined product.

To produce natural sugars, the harvested cane is split and fed through rollers to squeeze out the sugar juice, which is then cleaned and clarified. It is thickened by evaporation, boiled and seeded with tiny sugar crystals which grow in the syrup. Still coated with molasses, the large crystals are spun away, to produce, as it were, the first crop, demerara sugar.

The syrup is seeded and crystallized twice more. The product of the second crystallization is sold as bulk raw sugar to the refining industry. The next batch is transferred to tall sugar bins which filter the molasses, leaving behind soft, raw sugar. The dry, light-coloured sugar at the top of the bin is known as light muscovado; dark muscovado is taken from the centre and molasses sugar, black and sticky, from the bottom, where much of the molasses has settled.

Molasses, the dark, thick syrup, can in fact vary from mid-brown to black and has a concentrated, sweet flavour.

Both treacle and golden syrup are refined products. Treacle is refined from molasses and, although equally dark in colour, is less sweet. Golden syrup, thinner and light amber in colour, is a by-product of the sugar-refining process and, as such, not a health food at all.

Do not be taken in. Not all brown sugars are natural and unrefined. Many branded makes of both light and dark brown sugars are manufactured from white refined sugars artificially coloured with caramel and refined molasses. The way to tell is, as always, to read the label. Natural brown sugar will not have a list of ingredients, just the country of origin – such as Guyana, Barbados or Mauritius.

Using natural sugar

Natural sugars are not just sweet, each one has a characteristic flavour all its own.

Demerara sugar with its crunchy texture is good on cereals, in crumbles, shortbread and rock cakes and for cake, biscuit/cookie and pudding toppings. It can also be used to sweeten coffee.

Light muscovado sugar is soft and creamy-coloured with a mild flavour. It is suitable for the lightest of baking, even sponge cakes, and makes delicious meringues. Use it to sweeten fruit, for syrups and for preserving fruits.

Muscovado, or dark muscovado sugar, also called Barbados sugar, is soft, fine-grained and dark brown and rich in natural molasses. This is the one to choose for moist baked goods such as rich fruit cakes and gingerbread, for dark steamed puddings, confectionery such as 'old-fashioned' toffee and for some preserves – grapefruit marmalade and chutneys.

Molasses sugar, with its higher molasses content and even stronger flavour, tastes in the raw rather like a good treacle toffee. This too is good for rich fruit cakes, Christmas pudding and other dried-fruit specialities.

Molasses is used to flavour milk drinks, cakes and puddings and is combined with nuts as a filling for sweet pies. It is used in savoury dishes too – in Boston baked beans, black-bean soup and some casseroles of pork, beef or venison.

You can replace half the sugar in cakes and other baked goods with molasses. Reduce or omit any baking powder required, and, to offset the natural acidity of molasses, add 2.5 ml (½ teaspoon) bicarbonate of soda for each 250 g (8 oz) (⅔ cup) used. Reduce the liquid in the ingredients by 45 ml (3 tablespoons).

Boiling sugar

When sugar is boiled for confectionery, decoration and food colourings, its characteristics change in leaps and bounds as each successive temperature change is reached. Use demerara or light muscovado sugar. Heat it gently in a large pan, stirring slowly. Never allow it to boil until the sugar has dissolved, which can take up to 30 minutes. Once it boils, increase the heat and do not stir the sugar again. Dip a sugar thermometer first in hot water. Test the temperature of the sugar and, to prevent further increase, stand the pan in cold water.

Storage

Natural sugars are naturally moist. Store them in airtight containers in a cool place. If the sugar goes lumpy, break it into pieces and warm for a few minutes in the oven at the lowest setting. Break it up and cool completely before storing.

Sugar-boiling chart

Stage	Temperature	Uses
Thread	101 °C, 215 °F	Syrup for fruit salad, poaching fruits
Pearl	105 °C, 220 °F	Jams, fondant sweets
Soft ball	115 °C, 240 °F	Soft fudge sweets
Hard ball	126 °C, 260 °F	Hard fudge sweets
Crack	138 °C, 280 °F	Soft toffee and frostings
Hard crack	155 °C, 310 °F	Spun sugar decorations and hard toffee
Caramel	163 °C, 325 °F	Pralines, caramel coatings and decorations
Black jack	199 °C, 390 °F	To colour rich cakes and puddings and as gravy browning

Honey

Honey is a super-saturated solution of sugars made by bees from the nectar and pollen of flowers and plants. It contains dextrose, fructose, sucrose, higher sugars, proteins and traces of amino acids. As the sugars have already been converted by the bees in this natural refining process, honey is rapidly absorbed into the bloodstream and is therefore a source of instant energy.

Many factors affect the flavour and characteristics of the honey – the type of plants from which the nectar was obtained, the time of year, the amount of sunshine and the amount of heat and pressure used to extract the honey from the combs.

Honey is liquid in the hive but begins to crystallize and become granular at room temperature. It is usually sold in jars but is also available 'on the comb', in which form it is packed either in jars or wooden boxes. Thick, set honey can vary in colour from milky white to dark amber. The natural cloudiness is caused by the pollen. Clear honey, which has been heat-treated, is easier to use in cooking, and can range from the palest corn colour to a deep, glowing bronze.

Health-food shops have wide ranges of pure, local honeys which capture the flavour of the plants and almost the heady scent of each particular region. You could set out on a feast of honey-tasting, comparing lime blossom with alpine flowers, Scottish heather fragrance with French lavender, the thyme flowers from the Greek mountains with the citrus blossoms of Florida.

And again, check the labels. Price is an indicator too, of honeys which are not only blended ('the product of more than one country': nothing wrong with that) but also processed.

Pure honey will never normally develop moulds and bacteria will not grow in it – indeed in biblical times it was used as an antiseptic. Stored in a cool, dry place it will keep indefinitely (witness a recent archaeological find, when a jar of 5000-year-old honey was found in an Egyptian tomb in perfect condition).

Cooking with honey

Honey gives a delicious flavour and a moist texture in baking of all kinds. You can use it to replace an equal weight of sugar in yeast-raised doughs. In cakes, you can replace up to half the weight of sugar. For every 125 g (5 oz) (⅔ cup) sugar you replace you will need only 100 g (4 oz) (⅓ cup) honey and 10 ml (2 teaspoons) less liquid. To compensate for the natural acidity, add a pinch of bicarbonate of soda.

Brush honey on to poultry, joints of roast pork or ham for a sweet and attractive glaze and on to scones and breads before baking or as soon as they come out of the oven. Use honey in place of sugar when making a syrup for fruit salads and when poaching fruits. As it is sweeter than sugar you will need roughly half the weight of honey.

Sugar substitutes

Chemical substitutes for sugar are not health foods at all. The healthy way to sweeten a dish without using refined or raw sugar or honey – all of which are too quickly absorbed into the bloodstream – is to use fresh or preferably dried fruits. Dried fruits such as apricots and dates are packed with fibre and proteins – and, unfortunately, calories too.

Of the chemical sugar substitutes, cyclamates, an American discovery, which were first used in the USA in 1950 and in Britain in the 1960s, are now banned in both countries after animal experiments have shown a tendency for them to cause cancer in the bladder. Saccharin, or ortho-sulphobenzimide, which is 500–600 times sweeter than sugar, is also under suspicion, particularly in the USA, where its commercial use is limited by law.

The message does seem to be that a gradual adjustment to less sweet foods and a wider use of those that contain natural sugars is the only answer.

SALT

Fats, sugars and now salt: another ingredient we have been consuming in large quantities without giving a thought to the consequences. According to the most up-to-date medical studies, the consequences may be severe. A heavy excess of salt in the diet can contribute not only to hypertension – to which some 40 per cent of the population is said to be susceptible – but to heart disease and brain haemorrhage.

Of course, a certain amount of salt is essential. It helps to maintain the correct level of body fluids and aids the transmission of messages through the nervous system. Without salt, the body soon reaches a serious state of dehydration. Therefore it is not a question of eliminating salt altogether – a virtual impossibility anyway, since so many foods contain it – but of knowing exactly which foods have a high sodium content and then taking care to avoid dangerous excesses.

Salt, a natural mineral evaporated from sea water or extracted from underground rock layers (see glossary entry), is made up of two chemical elements, sodium and chloride. And it is the sodium, representing about 40 per cent of the total weight of the salt, that we have to watch.

For satisfactory functioning of the human body under normal conditions, a surprisingly low salt intake is required – a minimum of less than only 500 milligrams or, to put it another way, 200 milligrams of sodium – with higher levels for people doing strenuous manual work or living in very hot climates. And yet the average daily consumption of salt in the UK is 12 grams per person – that is 4.8 grams or 4,800 milligrams of sodium. In the USA, where the whole question of salt awareness is well under way, the consumption is falling quickly and encouragingly.

People who eat a high proportion of natural foods have a much greater chance of being on the right side of this 'average intake' statistic than those who fill their supermarket trolleys with masses of canned and processed foods, which, almost without exception, have an over-high salt content.

Happily, none of the medical authorities is suggesting (except in cases of severe illness) that we aim to cut our salt intake down to the unpalatable minimum level – it would be very hard-going indeed if we did. In Britain the Health Education Council recommends cutting down to a target maximum of 9 grams of salt per day – certainly on the generous side of our actual requirements. In the USA, the American Heart Foundation has recommended salt restriction at three levels: to 1,250 milligrams of salt (500 mg sodium) for patients with serious heart conditions; to 2.5 g salt (1 g sodium) for those suffering from severe hypertension, and to a 'mild restriction' of 5–7.5 g salt (2–3 g sodium) per day for others.

Salt awareness

The first step towards cutting down on salt intake is to become totally aware of how, when and in what form we take it – reaching almost without thinking for the salt cellar at table and the salt drum in the kitchen is only the tip of the iceberg. The list of the sodium content of everyday ingredients shown overleaf provides some useful pointers. Preparing and cooking food at home instead of buying it canned and ready prepared is something people who are interested in health foods and natural ingredients do anyway. This way you can control the amount of salt you use; by opening a can of vegetables or a packet of cereals, you cannot.

Sodium content of foods

expressed in milligrams per 100 g (approximately 4 oz)

Food   Mg sodium

Breakfast cereals
All-Bran	1670
cornflakes	1160
muesli	180
oatmeal, raw	33
Puffed Wheat	4
Rice Krispies	1110

Flour and flour products
wholewheat flour	3
wheatmeal 85% flour	4
white bread 72% flour	3
white self-raising flour	350
soya flour	1
wholewheat bread	540
Hovis bread	580
soda bread	410
white bread	540
rye crispbread biscuits/crackers	220
digestive biscuits	440
oatcakes	1230

Dairy products
fresh whole milk	50
Channel Island/extra rich milk	50
sterilized milk	50
UHT (long-life) milk	50
fresh skimmed milk	52
dried whole milk	440
dried skimmed milk	550
goat's milk	40
salted butter	870
unsalted butter	7
plain yoghurt	76
single cream	42
canned sterilized cream	56
Camembert-type cheese	1410
Cheddar cheese	610
Danish blue-type cheese	1420
cottage cheese	450
eggs	140

Meat and poultry
gammon bacon rashers	1180
streaky bacon rashers	1500
rump steak	51
salted silverside of beef (boiled)/corned beef	910
loin lamb chops	61
loin pork chops	56
veal fillet	110
leg or wing portion of chicken	50
lamb's kidney	220
calf's liver	93

Meat products
ham	1250
luncheon meat	1050
salami	1850

Fish and shellfish
cod fillets, raw	77
smoked cod	1170
fresh haddock, raw	120
plaice, raw	120
herring, raw	67
crab, boiled	370
prawns, boiled	1590
shrimps, boiled	3840

Fish products
tuna, canned, in oil	420
sardines, canned, in oil	650

Vegetables
runner beans, raw	2
butter/calico beans, boiled	16
red cabbage, raw	32
white cabbage, raw	7
carrots, raw	95
mushrooms, raw	9
fresh peas, raw	1
frozen peas, raw	3
dried peas, boiled	13
potatoes, raw	7
potatoes, baked in skins	6
sweetcorn, raw	1
tomatoes, raw	3

Sodium content of foods, continued

Vegetable products			
baked beans in tomato sauce	480	raisins, dried, raw	52
carrots, canned	280	raspberries, raw	3
peas, canned	230	sultanas, dried, raw	53
instant potato powder	1190		

Vegetable products
baked beans in tomato
  sauce — 480
carrots, canned — 280
peas, canned — 230
instant potato powder — 1190
sweetcorn kernels,
  canned — 310

Fruit
applies, dessert, raw — 2
apricots, fresh, raw — trace
    dried, raw — 56
bananas, raw — 1
dates, dried, raw — 5
figs, dried, raw — 87
grapes, black or white, raw — 2
olives, in brine — 2250
oranges, raw — 3
plums, dessert, raw — 2
prunes, dried, raw — 12

raisins, dried, raw — 52
raspberries, raw — 3
sultanas, dried, raw — 53

Nuts
almonds — 6
brazils — 2
coconut, fresh — 17
      desiccated — 28
hazelnuts — 3
peanuts, fresh — 6
    roasted and salted — 440

Sweeteners
demerara sugar — 6
honey — 11

Flavourings
curry powder — 450
yeast extract — 4500
meat extract — 4800
vinegar — 16

To cushion the blow of flavour loss when you cut down drastically on salt, use other flavourings to compensate. Instead of spooning in the salt when cooking vegetables – probably the average cook's most subconscious action – add the very minimum, just a pinch. Simmer the vegetables in very little water or stock or steam them, then toss them in chopped fresh herbs, sprinkle them with cider vinegar or lemon or orange juice, and for good measure add a few grindings of black pepper. Each of these tricks in fact produces vegetables more delicious than those cooked with just plain salt! Add a pinch of mace, coriander or turmeric to scrambled eggs; liquidize a generous handful of fresh herbs with vegetables for soup; step up the garlic in salad dressing and omit the salt; serve crisp fresh vegetables like shredded red cabbage or spring/green onions with cold poultry when once you might have reached for the pickles – in simple ways like these you can make a substantial contribution to cutting down on the family's salt intake without a single look of reproach.

Get used to reading the labels on the cans and packets you buy – or are tempted to buy – and remember that ingredients are listed in the order of quantity, greatest first. Those at the beginning of the list represent the greatest in volume terms. Under UK regulations where salt is included in the ingredients it must be listed. Thus a can of luncheon meat will have the equivalent of a flashing light to the salt-wary. But many foods which are sold unpacked – cooked meats, bacon and cheese for example – do not have to carry an ingredients breakdown. So you have to know what – in salt terms – you are buying. Also, when salt is part of a compound ingredient which makes up less than 25 per cent of the total food content it need not be stated.

Here is where an attentive ear in school chemistry lessons would have been useful.

To cut down on sodium, you have to be able to recognize it on food labels in all its various forms. And when letter and number identification codes are used to signify additives (E201 equals sodium sorbate and E211 in new UK labelling schemes indicates sodium benzoate) it begins to get a bit tricky. Local libraries and council offices will be able to give you a full list of additives and their codes. It is a long way round to selecting healthy food for your family, and a sign of the times, perhaps, that it has become necessary. It is a good idea for anyone belonging to a local organization —women's groups, parent-teacher's associations and so on — to get a list and pass it round the group on a discussion evening. In this way, salt awareness will be on the up and up, and salt intake on the decrease.

Just as there are sugar substitutes for those who adamantly refuse to get used to the taste of a cup of sugarless tea, so there are salt substitutes, as well as low-sodium products. The salt substitutes generally contain potassium salts in place of sodium chloride: look at the labels of the various brands and you will find potassium chloride, lactose and edible starch on one; potassium chloride, potassium glutamate, glutamic acid and calcium silicate on another; and potassium chloride, food starches and ammonium chloride on a third. Salt substitutes based on natural herbs and spices are now available, too.

Low-sodium salt products combine sodium chloride with other minerals and achieve an overall salty taste with a much reduced sodium content. One which blends sodium chloride with ground sesame seeds is particularly tasty as a condiment and a cooking medium.

GLOSSARY

Aduki or **adzuki bean** The small, round red beans are the dried seeds of a bushy plant native to Japan and also cultivated in China and Korea. To cook, pre-soak, then cook in unsalted, boiling water for 1–1½ hours. Use in salads, soups, stews and as a hot or cold purée.

Agar-agar A tasteless vegetable product made from edible seaweeds, this is used as a gelling agent in place of gelatine in vegetarian, Jewish and some Asian cookery. It is sold as threads and as off-white crystals in packets or small drums. Agar-agar is only partially soluble in water and should be simmered in boiling water for 5 minutes to dissolve. Use in sweet and savoury moulds, ice cream, mousse or marshmallows.

Alfalfa One of the oldest cultivated plants, alfalfa is a deep-rooted herb that was first grown in North Africa. The leaves, which are rich in manganese, can be used as a herbal tea. The seeds contain 19 per cent protein and are high in minerals and vitamins. You can buy alfalfa flour (use in the ratio one to five parts with wheat or other 'baking' flours) and alfalfa powder, to add to soups, stews and sauces. Use the seeds in muesli, salads, as crunchy topping or in savoury bread. Sprouting alfalfa seeds are good as salad, stir-fried and in casseroles (see page 40).

Almond There are two types of almond: sweet almonds, which are most widely used in cooking, and bitter almonds, from which almond oil is made. Sweet almonds are available in the shell, shelled, blanched – with the tough brown skin removed – and halved, chopped or ground to varying degrees of fineness. To cook, grill, roast or fry whole or ground almonds for a deeper flavour. Use in all kinds of baking, in salads, or to accompany fish (especially trout). Ground almonds make a good coating for deep-fried fritters and cream cheese balls and topping for cold sweet mousses.

Amino acids Of the hundreds of amino acids present in proteins, eight are known as 'essential' because they cannot be manufactured in the body. These are isoleucine, leucine, lysine, methionine, phenylalanine, threonine, tryptophan and valine. Young children need two more: arginine and listidine.

Apple, dried The only dried fruit to retain all its vitamin C content, dried apples are sold peeled, cored and thinly sliced into rings and as freeze-dried flakes. To cook rings, soak and poach in water or fruit juice for 20 minutes. Reconstitute flakes in hot water for apple sauce or purée. Use chopped dried apple rings in muesli or with, for example, cabbage and carrots in salads; or, cooked, in crumbles, pies, flans and compotes.

Apple juices Available in bottles, cans, cartons and one-serving cartons, apple juice is pasteurized to stop it fermenting – which would turn it into cider. Extra vitamin C is sometimes added to stop the juice oxidizing. You can buy sweetened or unsweetened juice, cloudy,

clear, still or sparkling. Use as a very good alternative to syrup for desserts, fruit salads and poaching fruits; with mineral water in refreshing drinks; or serve with muesli.

Apricot, dried Every 100 g (4 oz) (¾ cup) dried apricots contains 12 mg vitamin C, 4.8 g protein and 24 g dietary fibre – a health food indeed. Glowing orange in colour, dried apricots are sold stoned and whole, halved or in pieces; Turkish wild apricots, small, round and deep bronze, whole and unstoned. To cook, pre-soak and simmer in water or fruit juice (orange is best) for 20–30 minutes. Use raw and dry in muesli, salads, stuffings and baked goods. Use cooked in compotes, crumbles, pies or flans; with chicken and lamb casseroles, as garnish to grilled meat. Purée for ice cream, mouse, fruit fool and as a sauce to serve with fruits or meat.

Arachide oil see *peanut oil*

Asafoetida This somewhat bitter flavouring derives from the milky juice in the stem of giant fennel plants, *Ferula asafoetida* and *F. narthex* which are natives of Iran and Afghanistan. The juice dries to a solid dark brown block and can be bought in this form, when it needs soaking, or as a powder. Use as a spice in Southern Indian dishes of pulses, vegetables, pickles, fresh and dried fish. It is rarely used with meat.

Bamboo shoots Much used in Chinese cookery, bamboo shoots are cut – like huge asparagus – as soon as they push through the ground. They have a similar texture to carrots and young parsnips and a sweet, delicate flavour. They are sold sliced, in cans. To use, drain and rinse, then stir-fry with meat, fish or other vegetables, add to salads with bean sprouts or chop up to fill Chinese pancakes.

Banana, dried Skinned and halved bananas are dried and compressed into blocks which darken to mid-brown and are sold by weight, usually 225 g (8 oz). Wafer-thin banana slices are freeze-dried into crisp, brittle 'chips'. In both forms the flavour of the fruit is greatly intensified. To cook, separate the banana halves from the block, soak for 30 minutes and poach in water or fruit juice or chop – as dates – and use in baking and salads. Serve the 'chips' as a snack, in salads or in muesli.

Barley A small, whitish grain, barley is one of the oldest cereals and native to Mesopotamia. Barley groats are the whole grain and take 1½ hours to cook if pre-soaked overnight. Pot barley is the whole grain with only the husk removed, not to be confused with pearl barley which – like white rice – has most of the bran and germ processed out, with a consequent loss of nutrients. Cook pot barley as for brown rice, in boiling water for about 45 minutes. There is also a partly pre-cooked type which cooks in about 12 minutes. Use as brown rice, as an accompaniment, in pilaffs, in soups, salads, casseroles, and meat and vegetable stuffings.

Barley flakes The whole barley grains are rolled to produce large, lightweight flakes which can be eaten raw with other grains in muesli. Use as rolled oats, for porridge, as thickener in honey or treacle tart, in flapjacks, biscuits/cookies and scones.

Barley flour This flour, which is light in colour, has a low gluten content and therefore poor raising quality. To use, mix half and half with wheat flour for bread and scones with a slightly sweet flavour and soft texture.

Barley wine A strong beer sold in small bottles and brewed from malting barley and yeast, it is known as malt liquor in the USA.

Bay salt, see *salt*

Beancurd, see *tofu*

Bean sprout These familiar Chinese vegetables, with a shoot about 5 cm (2 inches) long, are the young shoots of dried mung beans. For method, see sprouting seeds, page 40. Bean sprouts are sold fresh or canned. To cook fresh, blanch briefly in boiling, salted water or steam or stir-fry for 2–3 minutes. Use raw in salads, raw or cooked as filling for Chinese pancakes, cooked as vegetable acccompaniment.

Bee brood Larvae of baby bees, rich in vitamins A and D and protein, are sold canned and considered a delicacy. To cook, toss in melted butter and fry or grill. Use as a garnish, for example with fried prawns and rice.

Bengal isinglass, see *agar-agar*

Black or **turtle bean** These small, oval, dried beans have shiny black skins but are whitish inside. They are usually served with the spicy sauces associated with African and South American cooking. To cook, pre-soak, then cook in boiling unsalted water for about 2 hours. Use in savoury dishes with rice; in soups, stews, casseroles and salads. Chinese fermented black beans do not need soaking.

Black-eyed bean, or **black-eyed pea** Small, white dried kidney beans with a black spot, they are a traditional ingredient of African and America's Deep South cuisine. To cook, pre-soak, then cook in boiling, unsalted water for about 2 hours. Use in Hoppin' John with rice, herbs and tomatoes; in casserole of pork and vegetable hotpot. The ground beans are used in Africa as a coffee substitute.

Borlotti or **rose cocoa bean** These brown, speckled beans cook to a floury consistency and are good for thickening soups. In Italian cooking they are casseroled with bacon and cinnamon, and served in a soup with ham and onions. To cook, pre-soak, then cook in boiling, unsalted water for about 2 hours. Use with ham, bacon or pork, and in soups and salads, especially with strips of Parma ham and melon.

Bouquet garni This is a mixture of fresh or dried herbs immersed in a dish to flavour the stock or sauce. Fresh herbs can be tied together for easy removal, dried ones tied into a piece of muslin or cheesecloth. Bouquets garnis can be bought ready-made. The usual components are a bay leaf, parsley and thyme with various additions such as celery leaves, basil and tarragon.

Bran The tough, outer coating of wheat or other grains, bran is rich in high-quality protein, B vitamins and phosphorus. It consists of dietary fibre in its most concentrated form and performs an invaluable task in providing bulk to transport food matter speedily through the intestines. Bran is milled out when grains are processed (for white flour, for example) and is sold as a soft, medium-brown coarse powder. To use, add it in small quantities to flour in all kinds of baking – bread, pastry, scones, cakes and biscuits/cookies; use as a main ingredient in muesli; sprinkle on soup, puddings; or thicken soups and sauce with it.

Brazil nut The large, creamy-white nuts have a subtle almost sweet and milky flavour. Once shelled, they should be stored in an airtight container; after about 3 months they develop an unpleasant bitterness. Use whole as a dessert, with dried fruits; with cereals, fruit salads, confectionery, in cakes, especially on top of fruit cake; sliced, chopped or ground, in baking. They can also be roasted or toasted.

Brewer's yeast Sold in powder or tablet form, this by-product of the brewing process contains all the B complex vitamins, especially B1 and B2, and is rich in phosphorus, iron and calcium. To use, add the powder to drinks and any kind of liquid, savoury dish such as soups and stews; take tablets as directed on the packet.

Broad or **fava bean** More familiar in Britain and the USA in their fresh or frozen form, dried broad beans are a staple food in South America and popular in Greece. They are dark greenish-brown and have a mealy flavour; in Brazil they are ground into flour to make flat, dry bread. To cook, pre-soak, then cook in boiling, unsalted water for about 2 hours. They are good in salad with chives, onion and herbs, in casseroles of pork and beef and in bacon soup.

Brown rice The whole grain, from which only the inedible husk has been removed, brown rice retains the bran and germ and therefore the protein, fat, minerals, B vitamins and dietary fibre. It has a more 'nutty' flavour and is less starchy than milled white rice. Served in the same meal as pulses – rice with lentils – it completes the group of essential amino acids. Cook in a large pan with plenty of boiling water, or simmer in twice its volume of liquid (1 cup of rice and 2 cups of water or stock) in a covered pan for 40–45 minutes. Use to accompany meat, fish and vegetable dishes; as pilaff with those ingredients, nuts, seeds, dried fruits, herbs and spices; in stuffings for meat, poultry and vegetables; in salads tossed with other foods and flavoured dressings. Brown rice

can also be used in sweet dishes, to make milk puddings, or with fresh and dried fruits, or as a mould.

Buckwheat A staple food of Russia and Poland, buckwheat is cooked and can be served like brown rice. The small, brown and almost heart-shaped seeds are encased in a tough, inedible husk which has to be removed. The grain is high in protein, phosphorus and potassium and contains most B vitamins. Cook in boiling water for 12–15 minutes. Use as for rice, as accompaniment, or in dishes with pulses, vegetables, meat and fish.

Roasted buckwheat, or kasha, has a more nutty flavour. To cook, simmer in boiling water or stock for 10 minutes, until the grains are fluffy. Use raw in salads, muesli and as addition to bread dough; or cooked in traditional Russian dishes with vegetables.

Buckwheat flour The grey, very finely ground flour contains no gluten and if used alone makes flat, crumbly loaves. Combined with high-gluten flours it gives a pleasant nutty flavour. The best-known dish is buckwheat *blinis*, thin crisp pancakes raised with yeast.

Buckwheat or *soba* **noodles** In Japan, where these are the most popular noodles, there are *soba-ya* restaurants – the oriental equivalent of spaghetti houses. Cook *soba* in plenty of boiling water for 8 minutes, until just tender, then drain, rinse and drain again. Use hot or cold, with a spicy sauce: seaweed, horseradish and raw onion are usual accompaniments.

Buckwheat spaghetti With a more delicate flavour than its wholewheat counterpart, the spaghetti is greyish-brown and the only whole-grain pasta which does not contain eggs. Cook in plenty of boiling, salted water for 10 minutes, drain, rinse under hot water and drain again. Use as other pasta. This is specially good with vegetable sauce.

Bulghar, burgul or **roasted wheat** The wheat grains are boiled, dried and roasted. To cook, simmer in twice their volume of liquid for 15 minutes. To use without further cooking, soak in water for 30 minutes to swell the grains. Dry thoroughly, toss with onion and herbs for tabbouleh salad, or mix with minced lamb for meatballs. Use cooked as other cereals, as accompaniment, or in soups and casseroles.

Butter, calico or **Madagascar bean** The beans grow in tropical regions and are native throughout America. Among the largest of the pulses, the dried beans are large and flat, shaped like broad beans but milky white. They are sold dried, and also cooked and canned. To cook, pre-soak, then boil in unsalted water for at least 1 hour. Use as an accompaniment to roast and grilled meat, especially bacon; in soups, casseroles and salads. Drain and rinse the canned beans, and serve in herb vinaigrette as an instant salad.

Buttermilk Originally the residue from the traditional butter-making process,

buttermilk is now made from pasteurized skimmed milk treated with a culture. It has a slightly sour taste, like yoghurt. Its acid content makes it ideal for use in scones. Use in baking; with muesli, as a drink; or it can be diluted with water, soda water or fruit juice.

Calcium Together with phosphorus, calcium is one of the major elements in bones. Hard water and dairy products such as milk and cheese are good sources. Vitamin D is needed to enable the body to absorb it.

Calico bean, see *butter bean*

Calories The actual definition of a calorie is the amount of heat needed to raise the temperature of 1 kg water 1 °C. But calories are better known to those who watch their body weight as the unit used to calculate the amount of food energy consumed and the amount of body energy expended. Both carbohydrates and proteins provide about 400 and fat 900 calories per 100 g (4 oz). Some of these are used up by the body, some in exercise, and any in excess are converted and stored as fat.

Candied fruits A method of preserving fruits of all kinds, by poaching them for a short interval each day in a heavy sugar or glucose and water syrup. All kinds of fruit can be treated in this way, and are popular especially at Christmas, wrapped in film or foil and packed in boxes. Plums, greengages, satsumas and apricots are some examples, while *marrons glacés*, the French chestnut delicacy, are the best-known. Use as a sweetmeat; chopped in ice cream and hot and cold desserts; sliced, for decorating cakes and puddings.

Candied peel The peel of citrus fruits, lemon, orange and citron, is treated in a similar way to whole fruits. It is best bought in large strips, which retain more flavour than the chopped, mixed type. To use, chop and add to fruit cakes and puddings, teabreads and scones. It is delicious in muesli. Or slice thinly and use as cake and pudding decoration.

Cannellini bean Native of Argentina, the beans are widely grown and used in Italy. Dried, they are like small, white kidney beans and are interchangeable with haricot beans. To cook, pre-soak and cook in boiling, unsalted water for 1–1¼ hours. Use as for haricot beans.

Carrageen moss, dulse, or **Irish moss** One of the most widely used sea vegetables in Britain, carrageen moss is collected from the Atlantic coast of Ireland and dried in the sun. It is used as a vegetarian setting agent in place of gelatine, and deep-fried as a delicacy. To use as a setting agent, soak 50 g (2 oz) moss in water for 15 minutes, wash and drain. Simmer in 1 litre (1¾ pint) (4½ cups) stock or fruit juice for 30 minutes. This will set 225 g (8 oz) chopped fruit or vegetables. Cool and leave in the refrigerator, soak, coat in batter and deep-fry; or sauté or stir-fry with vegetables.

Carob powder A low-fat chocolate substitute prepared from dried locust beans, this very fine brown powder looks and tastes like cocoa powder. It has a high natural sugar content and is therefore an efficient sweetener – and contains valuable B vitamins, calcium, phosphorus, iron and copper. It is also sold in blocks, like chocolate, which can be used for cake and dessert decorations.

Carbohydrates In the process known as photosynthesis, carbohydrates are manufactured in the green leaves of plants and are stored in seeds, fruits and roots. They are chemical substances made up of carbon, hydrogen and oxygen and all, except cellulose, are broken down in the human body into sugars. Together with fats, they are the body's main source of energy.

Cashew nut The nuts are always sold ready shelled, because they have to be high-temperature roasted to drive off a toxic oil between the shell and the kernel. They are shaped like long, pale cream kidney beans and sold whole, halved, broken and salted as snacks. Use in baking, salads, savoury stuffings, mixed with other nuts in savour 'loaves'; especially in pilaff and curry.

Channa, or **channa dal** Indian term for a dried pulse, a type of yellow pea.

Chestnuts Spanish or sweet chestnuts contain only about 2 per cent each of fat and protein. In spite of their apparent dryness, almost half their weight is water, which means they have the lowest calorific value of all nuts – 170 calories per 100 g (4 oz). In winter they are traditionally cooked in the shell over open fires to be peeled and eaten with salt. They are sold in the shell, whole and dried, cooked and canned, or as purée with and without sweetening. They are tedious to shell (see page 34). To cook, simmer in milk, water or stock or steam for about 1 hour. Use in stuffings, especially for turkey, with brussels sprouts as a vegetable accompaniment; the purée is served as 'mont blanc' in meringue cases and in desserts with chocolate. *Marrons glacés*, a French delicacy, are candied chestnuts.

Chick pea, or **garbanzo** Commercially grown in the USA, Africa and Australia, dried chick peas can be yellow, brown, red or black; the most common are beige and about the same size as shelled hazelnuts. In North Africa they feature in cous-cous dishes and in Greece and Turkey are served as a salad or cooked and ground to a paste with olive oil, as hummus. To cook, pre-soak and cook in boiling, unsalted water for about 3 hours. Use as a salad; as paste, savoury dip or spread; in soups, and meat and vegetable casseroles; as a vegetable accompaniment, especially with pork, bacon and rabbit.

Chilli bean, see *red kidney bean*

Cholesterol The human body manufactures all the cholesterol it needs – a fatty substance with neither taste nor smell. It is present in animal products and in the fruit and seeds of some plants – coconut and avocado pears, for example – in the form of saturated (or solid) fat. Excesses of cholesterol are thought by medical experts to be linked with heart disease. See section on fats and oils.

Cider vinegar Many claims are made for the health-giving properties of cider vinegar, which is widely used in homeopathic medicine. It is rich in potassium, phosphorus and calcium, and also contains iron, chlorine, sodium, magnesium, sulphur, fluoride, silicon and trace elements. The vinegar varies in colour from pale gold to deep amber; caramel is sometimes added to deepen the colour. Apart from replacing other vinegars in salad dressings and sauces, preserving and pickling, it can be taken medicinally. Mix 10 ml (2 teaspoons) in a glass of water and drink 2–3 times a day, or use as a gargle for sore throats and inflammation.

Cobnut, see *hazelnut*

Coconut The large fruit of the coconut palm, which grows in the tropics, consists of an outer fibrous and hairy husk inside which there is a wall of creamy white 'flesh' enclosing a sweet, chalky-white liquid, the 'milk'. The coconut flesh is uniquely high (in vegetable terms) in saturated fat, which is sold in blocks as coconut cream. The milk is low in calories and easy to digest. Coconut is sold whole and desiccated, or dried in shreds, long strands, chips and finely grated. It is also available as ready-toasted chips. Use in cake and meringue mixtures, as cake and dessert topping, stirred into or sprinkled on curry, pulse and rice dishes. Use coconut cream in spiced Indian and West Indian savoury dishes in place of oil. To make simulated coconut milk, soak desiccated coconut in boiling water for 30 minutes and press through a sieve.

Coconut oil Because it is high in saturated fatty acids and low in polyunsaturates (with only 2 per cent linoleic acid) coconut oil is the odd man out among vegetable oils. Use it sparingly, to brush a non-stick pan for stir-frying or mixed in small proportion to other oils.

Coffee substitutes Coffee contains a mild stimulant, caffeine, which gives some people unpleasant side-effects – insomnia particularly. Decaffeinated coffee is sold in beans, ground and granular forms and there are a number of substitutes based on other vegetable products. The best-known of these is dandelion root coffee (q.v.). Others can be made from grains – oats, millet, barley – sometimes mixed with molasses and bran.

Corn, sweetcorn or **maize** Wild corn originated in South America, where the modern hybridized strains are still a staple food. Different varieties of corn are cultivated for use as a vegetable, flour, meal, hominy grits, popcorn, oil (q.v.) and animal feed. Corn on the cob can be boiled or roast and eaten whole, spread with butter and seasoned with herbs: this way it is a barbecue special. You can strip kernels from the cobs, or buy them canned or frozen. Use to make creamy soups; with bacon and fish in chowders; in casseroles, pancakes, soufflés and as a vegetable accompaniment.

Cornmeal The meal can be yellow or white and is available finely or coarsely ground. It has a low gluten content and, unless mixed with other flour, makes hard, flat breads evocative of early America. It also has a slightly bitter after-taste. Cornmeal is used for Mexican tortillas and taco shells, both sold in cans to fill with spicy meat sauces. Polenta is the Italian corn meal and the Mexican version is known as *masa harina*. Store in an airtight tin for up to 2 months. Use with wheat or other flour in cornbread, muffins and buns, pancakes and as thickening.

Corn oil The oil pressed from corn kernels is sold in both unrefined – natural – and refined forms. It has about 60 per cent saturated fatty acids and 40 per cent linoleic acid, or polyunsaturated fats. It is widely used in the manufacture of margarine. The oil does not retain much of the characteristic of the grain and is chosen more on its relatively low price than on flavour. Use for frying, casseroles, to add to batter mixture, and in cakes.

Corn syrup Corn kernels are hydrolized to make corn syrup, which is widely used as a sweetener in the USA. It can be light or dark amber in colour; generally, the darker the syrup the less refined it is and the more flavour it has. In steamed puddings and baking corn syrup can replace up to half the sugar: use 600 ml (1 pint) (2½ cups) syrup for each 225 g (8 oz) (1 cup) sugar and reduce the liquid ingredients. Use also in confectionery, in sweet sauces and with waffles and pancakes.

Cottage cheese A low-fat soft cheese made from skimmed or partly skimmed milk, cottage cheese can contain as few as 96 calories per 100 g (4 oz) (½ cup). The large, soft curds are quickly formed when the milk is heated. As the cheese contains a high proportion of the liquid whey, it is permanently moist. Use in salads (it is especially good with bananas, oranges and dates); in cheesecakes, both sweet and savoury; in dips with flavourings such as avocado or anchovy; in sauces and toppings in place of higher-calorie cheese; as a garnish for cold soups; as a sandwich filling. Sieve the cheese when a smooth texture is needed.

Cous-cous The grains are produced from semolina made from hard durum wheat which is moistened, coated with fine flour and then 'exploded'. Cous-cous grains are light, volume for volume with other cereals. They are cooked by steaming over flavoured stock to serve with spicy meat and vegetable casseroles in the traditional North African manner. To cook, see page 71. Use as an accompaniment to meat, fish and vegetable dishes or with highly spiced sauces; as a dessert, sweetened with fruits and honey.

Cracked, crushed or **kibbled wheat** The whole wheat grain is coarsely ground to make a quicker-cooking cereal. To cook simmer in 2½ times its volume (1 cup cracked wheat to 2½ cups water or stock) for 20 minutes. To use, add small amounts raw to bread or scone dough, or sprinkle as a topping; use as an accompaniment or as rice in pilaffs and salads.

Cream cheese To be called cream cheese, the product must have a butterfat content of no less than 45 per cent, and double cream cheese must have 65 per cent (UK regulations). 'Full-fat soft cheese', sometimes wrongly described as cream cheese, has cream added to curds and may have a butterfat content of 10–15 per cent. The cheeses sold 'loose' in delicatessens or packed in tubs are unripened. Some of the most delicious and best-known cheese in the world – Brie and Camembert – are quick-ripening examples and Pont l'Eveque a brine-washed ripened cream cheese.

Crispbread A Scandinavian speciality, crispbreads are very light, wafer-thin biscuits/crackers made with rye flour or whole-wheat flour with added bran. The biscuits/crackers are eaten in place of bread for packed lunches, picnics, with soup and cheese. Weight for weight, they contain more calories than bread. Use with a variety of toppings as cocktail savouries and open sandwiches; crushed as garnish for soup; as a crispy topping for breads; or mixed with butter as no-cook 'pastry' base for savoury cheesecakes.

Crushed wheat see *cracked wheat*

Crystallized or **glacé fruits** Candied fruits (q.v.) are dried and given a hard surface of granulated sugar, or coated with more sugar which makes them shiny and ice-like. Crack off extra-thick sugar layers before cooking. Health-food shops sell diced and crystallized papaya, pineapple and melon as well as the more familiar tree fruits. Use as sweetmeats; chopped in cakes, puddings and ice creams; or sliced as decoration.

Crystal salt, see *salt*

Curd cheese, pot cheese, or **farmer's cheese** Made by straining the milk solids (the curds) from the liquid whey, this is the easiest cheese to make at home since it requires no further process, such as ripening. The German equivalent is called quark and the French version *fromage blanc*. Cottage cheese (q.v.) is a form of curd cheese. Use as for cream and cottage cheeses.

Currant The tiny, shrivelled and nearly-black fruits dried from Corinth grapes are in no way related to the soft red, black and white currants. In the USA, the dried fruits – not popularly used – are called Corinth raisins. Use in cakes, biscuits/cookies, sweet scones, tea bread, steamed and baked puddings; with cottage cheese as a pancake filling.

Often mixed with, and sometimes sold ready packed with, raisins and sultanas, as 'cake fruit'.

Dal, or **dhal** A generic word used in Indian cooking to describe lentils and split peas of all kinds. More specifically, a dish of lentils cooked with herbs and spices, which can be very liquid, and is served as a soup, or cooked until the water has evaporated, to make the thick purée that accompanies curry and/or rice.

Dandelion coffee A coffee substitute made from the soluble solids of roasted dandelion root, which is extracted commercially without the use of chemicals. It is available in powder or granules. As the compound is completely caffeine-free it is also suitable for late-night drinks. It is possible to make a passable version of dandelion coffee at home. Pull the plant roots in autumn, cut off the leaves and wash and dry the roots. Bake them in a cool oven until they are dried and crisp. Store in airtight containers, then chop and grind in a blender or food processor.

Dashi A clear, golden soup stock used in Japanese cooking. It is made with flakes of dried bonito fillet and dried seaweed and sold in cans or in powdered form. Use in Japanese soups, and in stews, sauces and casseroles. (Bonito is a fish of the mackerel family, similar to tunny fish.)

Dates, dried The date palm is one of the world's oldest fruits under cultivation. Shiny dark brown dates are sold fresh for a short season. Sun-dried ones are exported in boxes, whole and unstoned, as sweetmeats; stoned and loose or compressed into space-saving blocks. They need no cooking and can be chopped into muesli, or mixed with cottage or cream cheese or banana as a sandwich filling. Chopped dates make fruit cakes and puddings rich and moist; they are good layered between wholewheat pastry for date slice. Whole stoned dates filled with soft cheese, almond or apricot paste make quick and easy *petits fours*.

Date 'sugar' You can make a high-fibre sugar substitute from dried and ground dates. For method, see page 21. Use in place of natural sugars in baking, on cereals or in salad dressing.

Decaffeinated coffee, see *coffee*

Demerara sugar This type of brown sugar was first produced in the Demerara county of Guyana. It is a natural sugar with a sticky texture and the rich aroma of the natural molasses it contains. It has large, clear, sparkling crystals. Use to sweeten coffee; on cereals; as a crunchy topping on baked foods; in scones, rock cakes and biscuits/cookies.

Desiccated coconut, see *coconut*

Dhal, See *dal*

Dietary fibre, See *fibre*

Dried fruits Dried tree and vine fruits are a valuable source of nutrients in a compact and convenient form – the perfect instant snack. They have endless

uses in sweet and savoury dishes and as sugar substitutes. (See separate entries, also dried fruit section, pages 8–25.)

Dried mushrooms With fresh field and cultivated mushrooms available all year round, dried mushrooms are scarcely needed in Western cooking. For Chinese and Japanese dishes, however, they are invaluable if all the various flavours of the different species are to be experienced. Additionally, fresh mushrooms are rarely used in China, since the flavour of dried ones is preferred. To reconstitute, remove the tough stems and use for soup. Soak the caps in tepid water for 20 minutes. Drain and pat dry. To cook, boil in soup; slice and stir-fry; or braise with other vegetables.

Dulse, see *carrageen moss*

Durum wheat A 'hard' wheat grown in the USA and used mainly to make wholewheat pasta.

Egg noodles Almost every country has its own regionally characteristic version of noodles, which are made from a flour, egg and water paste. The paste is cut into long, thin ribbon strips and compressed into loosely packed blocks or bundles, sold either fresh or dried. Some types are pre-cooked by steaming, to cut down on cooking time. To cook, follow specific directions according to type. Use as an accompaniment; with meat, fish or vegetable sauces; in clear soups and casseroles, and with dried fruits and sweet sauces.

Endosperm The endosperm makes up about 90 per cent of wheat and other grains and consists mainly of starch. This is virtually all that is left when the bran and germ are milled out, as for white flour and polished white rice.

Farmer's cheese, see *curd cheese*

Fava bean, see *broad bean*

Fibre, or **dietary fibre** Dietary fibre is the substance that forms the cell wall and rigid structure of all plant foods. In the Western world the average daily intake of fibre is only about 20 g (⅔ oz), but the recommended quantity for good health is 30–35 g (1–1¼ oz) per day. Shortfall in dietary fibre is now considered to be a major factor in many prevalent diseases and ailments – coronary heart disease, large bowel cancer, appendicitis, diverticular disease of the colon, gallstones, diabetes, obesity, haemorrhoids, varicose veins and tooth decay.

Whole grains and whole-grain products – flour, semolina, pasta – are good sources of fibre. For example a 50 g (2 oz) slice of wholewheat bread contains 4 g (⅕ oz) fibre, against 1 g (1/20 oz) in white bread. Legumes and all dried pulses are high-fibre foods – 50 g (2 oz) (⅓ cup) kidney beans provides 4 g (⅕ oz) fibre. And so are dried fruits and nuts. The same weight of uncooked dried apricots contains 12 g (½ oz) fibre, or one-third the recommended daily intake; the same weight of almonds contains 7.15 g (¼ oz).

By including plenty of whole grains, pulses, dried fruits, nuts, fresh fruits and vegetables in our diet we can improve our health and benefit from the outcome of years of meticulous medical research.

Figs, dried Whole dried figs are sold either packed in decorative gift-boxes, as sweetmeats, and, more cheaply, loose or in packets. They are equally delicious either way. It is also possible to buy them compressed, either in blocks or as a paste. Dried figs can be eaten raw and chopped into cake mixes without pre-cooking. To cook, as a compote alone or with other dried fruits, pre-soak, then simmer in water or fruit juice for 20–30 minutes.

Filbert, see *hazelnut*

Five-spice powder A ready-made spice mix, sold in small quantities in packets, consisting of ground star anise seeds, fennel seeds, cinnamon, cloves and cardamom seeds. Use a pinch or so at a time – to taste – to season 'red-cooked' meats and poultry.

Flageolet Considered by many to be the 'king' of dried pulses, this bean is harvested when it is very young and pale green. Flageolets are widely grown and used in France – where the name means flute – and Italy. To cook, pre-soak, then cook in boiling, unsalted water for about 1½ hours. They make a very good accompaniment to lamb, especially cooked with it in a casserole; use also in soups and salads with fresh herbs and spring/green onion.

Foules mesdames bean These small, round, brown dried beans, grown in Egypt, are popular in Middle Eastern dishes. They have a somewhat earthy taste. To cook, pre-soak, then cook in boiling, unsalted water for about 1½ hours. Use in salads, with garlic dressing, or cooked in meat stock as soup, or in casseroles and stews.

Fromage blanc A cheese made from milk or skimmed milk, brought to blood heat and then set with a few drops of a cheese culture. It looks and tastes like thick yoghurt. In France it is served as a dessert topped with thick cream, sugar or honey. Serve in place of cream, or yoghurt, with fruit and cereals.

Garam masala An aromatic mixture of ground spices used throughout India as a condiment, or added to curries and kebab dishes towards the end of the cooking time. Its purpose is to add extra piquancy or form a spicy crust to bland ingredients. Unlike curry powder, it is not usually stirred in at the beginning. A typical mixture includes ground black pepper, cumin, cloves, cinnamon, mace, cardamom and coriander. Use as described, in very small amounts; sprinkle a pinch of the spice mix on yoghurt salad.

Garbanzo, see *chick pea*

Garlic This plant is a member of the onion family, *Allium sativum*, which is thought to have originated in Asia, though its earliest uses pre-date history. Each bulb is divided into many sections, or cloves, each one covered in a thin, papery skin. The size, colour and flavour of the bulb differ according to the variety – some are pure white and others purple, some almost sweet and others very pungent. Garlic is thought to reduce blood pressure and aid digestion.

As a flavouring, garlic has a place in every savoury dish, fried in the oil before stir-frying meat, fish and vegetables; in soups, stews, casseroles, and tomato and other sauces. Slivers of garlic can be pushed into meat – lamb particularly – before cooking, and a clove can be rubbed round a salad bowl for a subtle flavour, or infused in the dressing.

You can also buy minced garlic, freeze-dried flakes and garlic-flavoured salt and pepper.

Germ The germ represents only about 2 per cent of the total grain, be it wheat, rice or whatever, but in health terms it is disproportionately important. It is the germ that contains the minerals, vitamins and protein. And it is the germ that is milled out to convert natural whole grains into milled, polished (and nutritionally diminished) 'white' grains.

Both wheatgerm and oat germ are sold in health food shops as soft, light, mid-brown substances. Germ should be stored in a covered container in the refrigerator. Add them to whole grains and cereal flakes in muesli; add 30–45 ml (2–3 tablespoons) germ to bread, cake and biscuit/cookie dough; sprinkle in soups and casseroles, on baked puddings and porridge.

Ghee This is clarified butter, the usual frying medium in Indian cooking, which has a higher flash-point than whole butter. You can buy it in cans or prepare it at home. For the latter, melt butter in a pan and when it separates pour it through a strainer lined with muslin. Cool, cover and refrigerate the clarified butter and discard the foamy solids. Use for shallow frying in place of butter, margarine and oil.

Ginger One of the first spices brought to Europe by Arab merchants, ginger is indigenous to Asia and is grown in tropical regions of India, China and Japan. It is available in many forms and has widely differing uses.

Fresh ('green') root ginger is sometimes obtainable in health-food shops and Oriental grocers. Store it wrapped in foil in the refrigerator for up to 3 weeks. Peel and grate or slice it, to fry with stir-fried vegetables or meat, or use it to flavour steamed fish. It is also sold sliced and canned. Dried root ginger, like knobbly Jerusalem artichokes, is used in the same way. Peel and lightly crush a piece and infuse it in stewed fruit or preserves, or in vinegar for pickling. The dried root is ground and sold as a powdered spice, for use in baking and, with other spices, in curried dishes.

Preserved ginger is the fresh root steeped in syrup and sold in jars to use as a sweetmeat; or it can be sliced and added to fruit compote. Crystallized ginger can be used in cakes, puddings and ice cream. Ginger essence is used in confectionery and desserts.

Ginseng An ancient Chinese medicine which is now widely available and highly regarded in the West, ginseng is derived from the root of *Panax ginseng*. It has been found to contain six glycosides, or panaxosides, as well as amino acids, organic acids, sterols, flavanoids and vitamins. However unfamiliar these 'ingredients' may seem, the soothing and preventative properties of the root are well documented. Ginseng is sold as a powder, and in extract and tablet form.

Glacé fruits, see *crystallized fruits*

Glucose Present in plants such as onions and sweetcorn, glucose, a natural sugar, is formed in the body when other carbohydrates are digested. It is sold in the form of powder, between icing/powdered and caster/granulated sugar in texture, and liquid and can be used in place of sugar and honey for sweetening. As a rough guide, it has about half the sweetening capacity of sugar. Powdered glucose is used in confectionery, especially for candied fruits.

Granola A breakfast mix of cereal grains, seeds and nuts, granola is similar to muesli. It is sometimes sweetened with raw sugar or honey and lightly spiced with vanilla or ground anise. The term is also used to describe muesli-type cereals which have been tossed in melted oil, sugar and honey and lightly toasted. As a guide, allow 30 ml (2 tablespoons) oil and 15 ml (1 tablespoon) each of light muscovado sugar and clear honey to each 175 g (6 oz) (1½ cups) of the cereal. Spread on a baking tray and cook in the oven at 180 °C, 350 °F, Gas 4 for 20 minutes, turning frequently. Cool and store in a covered container.

Green tea, see *gunpowder tea*

Grits, see *hominy grits* and *soya grits grits*

Groats Whole grains (of wheat, oats, barley, rye and so on) are referred to as groats, and also as 'berries', therefore 'wheat groats' and 'wheat berries' are synonymous terms.

Groundnut oil, see *peanut oil*

Gungo or **pigeon pea** Small, dull-brown, dried seeds used in West African and West Indian dishes, these feature prominently in 'soul food'. To cook, pre-soak, then cook in boiling, unsalted water for at least 2 hours. Use particularly with highly spiced sauces and with rice.

Gunpowder or **green tea** A high-quality China tea with a pronounced green colour and a distinctive, slightly peppery, flavour.

Haricot or **navy bean** These small, creamy-white, dried beans, a variety of kidney bean, are indigenous to Central and South America. They are probably most familiar as the standard ingredient in baked beans. To cook, pre-soak, then cook in boiling, unsalted water for 1–1½ hours. Use with tomato sauce as accompaniment; as baked beans, for snacks; in soups and casseroles; or puréed.

Hazelnut also **filbert, Kentish cob and cobnut)** The shells are round or oval and crack easily to release the small nuts encased in a light, papery, brown skin. Hazelnuts are high in vitamin B1, phosphorus, copper and magnesium and contain about 40 per cent water. You can buy them in shell, shelled and whole or ground. Toast the nuts or ground nuts to increase the flavour. Use whole in muesli, salads, confectionery, chopped or ground in cakes, meringue, pastry and as topping for desserts such as mousses and cold soufflés. Filberts and Kentish cobs are related types of nut.

Herbal teas, see *tisanes*

Hiziki A seaweed which is cut into long, thin strands and looks rather like spaghetti. It can be served boiled, as an accompaniment.

Hominy, or **hominy grits** The large, starchy endosperm of the corn, or maize, kernel is cooked and crushed or ground to form 'grits', a staple food in early American households. It is sold ready-cooked in cans, needing only to be re-heated, or in packets. To cook packaged hominy, boil in 4 times its volume of water for about 1 hour (follow packet instructions). Use as porridge, with sugar, corn or maple syrup, honey, butter or milk; or as a bacon-and-egg accompaniment. Cold hominy can be sliced and fried, which makes it resemble corncakes.

Honey For centuries honey has been credited with almost mystical properties and its supposed healing powers are legendary. It contains vitamins B1, B2 and B3, pantothenic acid, B6, biotin and folic acid and – depending on the type – can be high in vitamin C. Its mineral composition includes iron, copper, sodium, potassium, manganese, calcium, magnesium and phosphorus, and it contains several enzymes.

As the bee has already digested the nectar from which honey is produced, honey is a rapid source of energy as it goes straight into the bloodstream. The kidneys can more easily process honey than sugar and it is non-irritating to the lining of the digestive tract.

The flavour and colour of honey vary considerably according to the climate and type of plant – lime blossom, heather, thyme all have distinctive characteristics. To cook and use, see page 108. Honeycombs or cut sections of comb, with the honey contained in the waxy hexagonal cells, are a luxury teatime spread; also, honeycomb is sometimes taken to relieve hay fever. Honey cappings, the top layer of wax, have similar uses.

Indian nut, see *pine nut*

Iodized salt, see *salt*

Irish moss, see *carrageen moss*

Jumbo oats Rolled whole oat grains come in two sizes: these are the large ones. To cook, simmer in water for 25–30 minutes to make porridge, and serve with honey, yoghurt or buttermilk. Or use raw with other cereals in muesli.

Kafir, see *sorghum*

Kasha, see *buckwheat*

Kelp A member of the seaweed family, kelp is sold mainly in powder and tablet form. This sea plant, which grows at the bottom of the ocean, is high in vitamins, particularly A, B1, B2, B12, C and D1 and in iodine. It also has 20 amino acids and 60 trace elements. To use, add small quantities of the powder, which is virtually tasteless, to soups, stews and casseroles.

Kentish cob, see *hazelnut*

Kibbled wheat, see *cracked wheat*

Kidney beans, see *red kidney beans* and other individual entries

Konbu A type of seaweed, related to kelp, sold in thick green strands. It can be boiled and served as an accompaniment.

Laver and **laverbread** A red edible seaweed, laver is gathered along the coastline of Wales and Ireland. It is sold washed, boiled to a purée and ready to use, in which form it is known as laverbread. It is rich in vitmains and minerals, especially iron and protein, but low in fat. It is served as a vegetable.

Legume Any vegetable of the bean or pea family, both dried and fresh.

Lentil Among all dried pulses, lentils are second only to soya beans in their protein content. They are leguminous seeds, smaller than peas, which were first cultivated in the Orient. They vary considerably in colour, from white through all shades of yellow, brown, orange, red and pink to the slate-grey puy lentils. In Indian cookery, *malika masoor* refers to pink lentils; *masur* to red ones; *motth* to a round brown variety; and *urd* to black or white seeds. Unlike other pulses, lentils do not need pre-soaking. Cook them in boiling water for about 1 hour. The orange, or Egyptian, lentils cook to a mash; many others hold their shape and texture, but with some 60 varieties used in Indian cooking alone, it is impossible to generalize. Use in soups; as a spiced purée; fry cold, thick purée as spice cakes; serve as a vegetable accompaniment; or use to add texture to, or to thicken, casseroles.

Licorice root The root of a small perennial plant grown in Southern Europe and the Middle East, licorice has a strong, slightly sweet flavour with a bitter after-taste. This does not deter children from chewing the long, woody, pencil-like roots. Ground licorice powder can be used sparingly in milk drinks and puddings and is used to make shiny-black, rubbery-textured sweets.

Linseed Mainly cultivated for the oil they contain (linseed oil is traditionally used to season cricket bats and furniture, the small, shiny-brown oval seeds are relatively new on the health-food scene. Use in muesli, cakes, bread and biscuits/ cookies. The seeds are virtually tasteless.

An interesting footnote: birds will not touch them!

Locust bean Something chewy to chew! Locust bean pods grow to about 30 cm (12 inches) long and almost 2.5 cm (1 inch) wide. When dried, they are hard and brownish-black with a flavour something like dates. The sparse, small brown seeds are inedible. Use the beans as a snack or chopped in muesli. Soak and chop into cakes and teabread. (Never include the seeds.) The kernels are ground and used in the manufacture of imitation egg white for commercial meringues.

Low-calorie spread A type of soft, spreadable margarine which is made by blending saturated fats with water. If you prefer to buy a soft, polyunsaturated margarine, check the label.

Low-sodium salt Salt substitutes abound, as awareness that a high sodium intake can be harmful spreads. Low-sodium salt products contains potassium chloride, lactose and edible starch. They look and taste like table salt, but have a far lower sodium content – and are much more expensive. See pages 109–12.

Macadamia nuts Native to Australia, these nuts look like hazelnuts but are slightly larger. They have a high fat content of over 70 per cent and are certainly not a snack for slimmers.

Madagascar bean, see *butter bean*

Maize, see *corn*

Maldon salt, see *salt*

Malt extract The extract is made from malted barley and contains almost 50 per cent sugar – which is why it is considered an energy boost. It is sold mixed with cod liver oil – high in vitamins A and D – as a thick, brown, syrupy substance called cod liver oil and malt.

Malt liquor, see *barley wine*

Malt vinegar, see *vinegar*

Maple syrup 'The real thing', the processed sap of the maple tree, is very expensive, though there are many cheaper taste-alike products. Maple syrup is a deep golden brown, more liquid than treacle and sold in bottles, not cans. Use with cereals, waffles and pancakes; as a pouring sauce for ice cream; to sweeten cakes and puddings; to glaze ham, bacon and chicken; to sweeten baked beans; or to candy sweet potatoes.

Margarine This multi-purpose spread and cooking fat had humble beginnings: a French chemist manufactured it from beef fat extract, water and skimmed milk just over a century ago. Later it was made from hydrogenated vegetable or fish oils – but still entirely from saturated fats. Soft margarine, made with a high proportion of polyunsaturated fat, was invented as recently as the 1960s. Check the labels if you want to count the unsaturates. In soft margarine they can vary from about 60 to 80 per cent.

Masa harina, see *cornmeal*

Mead This traditional English drink is made by fermenting diluted honey and contains mallic acid. Whether or not it lives up to claims of combating gout and rheumatism, it makes a pleasantly sweet, strong alcoholic drink.

Mekabu seaweed A Japanese lobe-leafed seaweed, sold dried in curled strands. It must be pre-soaked. Use in soups and salads and as a garnish.

Melon seed Anyone can prepare melon seeds. Scoop the flat, oval seeds from the fruit, wash and dry and spread them on a baking tray to dry in a cool oven. Cool and store in an airtight container. Use in muesli, as a snack, in salads, or as a garnish.

Milk The proteins in milk contain all the essential amino acids and so it is virtually the ideal food. It has carbohydrates, calcium, vitamins A, B and C and most of the necessary minerals and salts. It is sold in many forms.

Homogenized milk is heat-processed to distribute the fat globules evenly, then it is pasteurized.

Pasteurized milk is heated then quickly cooled, and the cream rises to the top.

Skimmed milk has the cream layer skimmed off and is therefore lower in fat content and calories.

Dried milk powder is produced from concentrated homogenized milk; it loses thiamine, vitamin B12 and vitamin C in the process.

Dried skimmed milk powder is almost fat-free and popular with slimmers. It is useful for making low-fat yoghurt.

Ultra heat-treated milk, or UHT, or 'long-life' milk, is heated to a very high temperature and stays fresh for several months without refrigeration.

Goat's milk is more easily digestible than cow's milk because it has smaller fat globules. It is thicker and richer and makes excellent yoghurt. It is sold both fresh and frozen.

Millet Familiar as long stems of closely-packed seeds pushed between the bars of bird-cages, millet is a staple food in many parts of Asia and Africa. The tiny, pale yellow seeds can be added dry to muesli; or used as topping for baked foods or with oats in flapjacks. To cook, soak, drain and cook in boiling water for about 30 minutes. Serve as rice.

Millet flour As the grain is a staple in Ethiopia, the tough, flat, national bread (*injera*) is made from millet flour. For a softer texture, mix up to half millet flour with a high-gluten type of flour. Use to thicken sauces, soups or casseroles.

Minerals It was discovered only comparatively recently, in the 1950s, that in their way minerals are just as essential to good bodily health as fats, carbohydrates and proteins. The major essential minerals are calcium, found in milk, cheese and 'hard' water; phosphorus, from whole cereal grains and soya, for example; iron, from liver and eggs; magnesium, from cereals, pulses, green vegetables and fish; potassium, from meat, milk and green vegetables; sulphur, from meat, fish, eggs and brassicas; and sodium and chlorine from a wide range of foods.

Many other minerals present in food are essential, but only in minute quantities. These, called trace elements, are iodine, fluorine, zinc, copper, manganese, chromium, cobalt and molybdenum.

Mineral water 'Boiled waters' are available in both still and sparkling types. The different brands vary considerably in the mineral salt content, from about 35 mg to nearly 3000 mg per 1 litre (1¾ pints) (4½ cups). If you wish to follow a low-salt regime, check the labels and choose the brands with the lowest sodium levels. Use as a regular daily drink. Water serves to carry the nutritive elements around the body and helps in the elimination of waste. It is also good mixed with concentrated fruit juices, to dilute wine (as in France) and in pancake batter.

Miso, see *soya paste*

Molasses The thick, dark syrup which is left when both natural brown and refined sugars are taken off (see entry on sugar). It is sold in tins, and looks rather like black treacle. Molasses is a rich source of nutrients, including vitamin B6 and inositol, and the minerals iron, copper, calcium, phosphorus and potassium. Use in hot milk drinks and sweet sauces; to sweeten meat dishes such as pork and beans; in cakes and bread in place of honey.

Molasses sugar This is the blackest and stickiest of the raw, natural sugars, with a strong, toffee-like flavour. Use in dark, rich cakes and puddings and black toffee.

Monosodium glutamate (MSG) A salt of glutamic acid which is virtually without flavour but has the facility of enhancing the taste of other ingredients, especially meat. It is widely used in Chinese and Japanese cooking and is sometimes referred to as 'gourmet powder'.

Mono-unsaturated fats Unsaturated fatty acids are the ones which are liquid at room temperature and consist mainly of vegetable and fish oils. (For the purpose of definition, those fatty acids which have less than a full quota of hydrogen atoms and have carbon atoms joined together by only one double bond are termed mono-unsaturated.) They do not affect the cholesterol level of the blood one way or the other. Olive oil is an example of a fat high in oleic acid, the mono-unsaturated fat.

MSG, see *monosodium glutamate*

Muesli This breakfast cereal was devised at the beginning of the century by Dr Bircher-Benner, a Swiss physician, at his clinic. In his opinion a mixture of rolled oats, raw apple, hazelnuts, lemon juice and milk was the perfect food to start the day. Subsequent medical knowledge has greatly reinforced his belief. Now all cereal mixtures of cereal flakes, seeds, nuts, fresh and dried fruits are generically termed muesli.

Mulberry, dried A recent addition to the shelves of health-food shops, dried white mulberries from Turkey have the flavour of sultanas and can be used as these and other vine fruits. Because of their attractive appearance, light brown and with the characteristic seed formation (rather like small longanberries) they are specially good in muesli and salad.

Mung bean Small, round and bright green, this dried bean has a sweet flavour and tastes and looks rather like miniature *petit pois* when cooked. It is native to India and is also grown in China, Africa, the USA and Australia. Mung beans are sprouted to produce the familiar Chinese bean sprouts, which are rich in vitamin C. To cook the beans, pre-soak, then cook in boiling, unsalted water for up to 1 hour. Use where their appearance will be an advantage: in salads; as an accompaniment; or tossed with rice.

Muscatel Dried from the muscat variety of grape, muscatels are deep purplish-black with large pips. Grown in the Malaga region of Spain, in Australia and South Africa, they are sold mainly for dessert, and are traditionally soaked in brandy ('preserved' is a misleading term, as the dried fruit is adequately preserved by the drying process). See recipe, page 19.

Muscovado sugar Raw, natural and unrefined cane sugar, sold as 'light' and 'dark' muscovado sugar, is produced in the West Indies in Barbados, Mauritius and Guyana. The natural sugar contains the important trace elements of minerals. See pages 105–6.

Navy bean, see *haricot bean*

Noodles In China, noodles are a symbol of longevity and as such are often served at birthday celebrations. They are long, thin strips of paste, which are sold fresh but more often dried. Chinese noodles are made of rice flour in flat strands, called rice sticks, and very thin round strips, called rice vermicelli. Transparent, or cellophane, noodles are made of mung bean, starch, pea starch or wheat. Italian noodles are made of durum wheat semolina; green noodles have spinach purée added. All noodles are served as a main dish with sauce; as accompaniment; in soup; added to casseroles. Cook according to individual directions until just tender.

Nori Sold in thin sheets, nori is a seaweed which is served, particularly in Japanese cooking, as a vegetable accompaniment.

Nuts, see *cashew, coconut,* and other individual entries

Oat bran and **oat germ** A stabilized product extracted from oat grains, this contains 16.25 per cent protein and 3.5 per cent dietary fibre. To make porridge for two, sprinkle 45 ml (3 tablespoons) on to 300 ml (½ pint) (1¼ cups) cold water, bring to the boil and boil for 3 minutes, stirring constantly. Serve with honey or sprinkled with chopped nuts. Use the product in muesli; stirred into yoghurt; to thicken soups, stews and casseroles; and in pastry, in proportion 50 g

(2 oz) (⅔ cup) to 150 g (6 oz) (1 cup) flour.

Oat flakes Rolled oats, or oat flakes, are produced from whole oats; one type is made from oats first softened by steam, then rolled to flatten them, cooled and dried. Quick porridge oats are rolled, partially cooked, cooled and dried. Cook rolled oats in three times their volume of water (1 cup oat flakes to 3 cups water) for 20 minutes. Oat flakes are the foundation on which muesli is built. Use them also in biscuits/cookies, especially oatcakes and flapjacks; in crumble toppings; in the proportion 50 g (2 oz) flakes to 150 g (6 oz) flour for crumbly pastry; or as a topping for bread.

Oatmeal Whole oats are ground to make a meal which can be fine, medium or coarse in texture. The coarsest grade, sometimes known as pinhead oats, should be soaked overnight. They can be cooked as porridge. Medium-grade oatmeal is also good for porridge and in oatcakes, biscuits/cookies, and added to pastry in the proportion of 50 g (2 oz) (⅔ cup) to 150 g (6 oz) (1 cup) flour. Fine oatmeal can be used in the same proportion as high-gluten flour in bread and scone dough and in crumble toppings; in muesli and to coat herrings for frying.

Oats Whole oats contain more protein and thiamine than any other grains, a little fat, and significant amounts of iron and potassium. The crop can be grown in harsh northern climates, where a bowl of porridge is still a warm and welcoming start to the day. Oat flakes (see above) are the main ingredient in muesli.

Oils Analysis of the levels of polyunsaturated, mono-unsaturated and saturated fatty acids in vegetable oils makes it possible to chart a 'health' graph. Coconut oil would have the lowest rating, with only 2 per cent of the 'good' linoleic polyunsaturated fat and a high level of saturated fat; olive oil next, with 10 per cent, though the remaining fat is largely the harmless mono-unsaturated type; then peanut oil, with 30 per cent linoleic acid; corn and sesame oils, with 40 per cent, and soya, safflower and sunflower oils at the top, all with 60 per cent.

Olive oil Unlike other vegetable oils, olive oil is mainly rich in oleic acid, the mono-unsaturated fatty acid. This means that it is easily digestible, and aids the absorption of the fat soluble vitamins A, D, E and K. It has only 10 per cent linoleic acid, the polyunsaturate, and for this reason could ideally be blended with, say, safflower oil for a better balance.

Olive oil has a very pronounced flavour which can even dominate other ingredients in some dishes. It is exported mainly by Greece, Italy and Spain and the produce of each country has its own characteristics. Check the label: quality varies. Cold-pressed oil is the natural and unrefined product and 'virgin' oil means that it is from the first pressing. Use in salad dressings, in pastes such as hummus (see recipe on page 44), for

stir-frying, or to fry-start casseroles. It has low-level smoking- and flashpoints at 170 °C, 325 °F and 285 °C, 545 °F respectively.

Orange-flower water One of the most heady and evocative of flavourings, orange-flower water is made by macerating the blossom to draw out the flavour. It is a clear, colourless liquid, sold in small bottles, and sometimes 'loose', by pharmacists. Use to flavour ice cream, sorbets, custard-type puddings, cakes, biscuits/cookies, confectionery, fruit compote, fruit sauce.

Organic growing Often fruit and vegetables in health-food shops are described as 'organically grown'. This signifies that they have been produced only with the use of natural fertilizers – compost from decayed and recycled plant matter, herbicides and what is descriptively termed farmyard manure. Products bearing this label should not have been sprayed with pesticides, nor grown in ground treated with chemical fertilizers. Organically grown fruit and vegetables are almost invariably more expensive, because in many cases they are grown privately, on small-scale holdings rather than in the massive co-operatives, and usually, without chemicals, the yield per acre is lower.

Peach, dried Dried peaches are a good source of iron. They are sold halved and are wrinkled, tough and greenish-yellow. They lose flavour in the process and benefit from being soaked in fruit juice – orange juice, or water flavoured with orange-flower water. Then they are delicious. To cook, simmer in soaking liquid, perhaps with added spices, for about 20 minutes. Use in compotes of mixed dried fruits; in pies, crumbles and flans; in casseroles; on kebabs with meat, poultry or fish.

Peanut or **groundnut** or **earth nut** Native to South America, peanuts are contained in the pods of a leguminous plant and have the unusual habit of pushing down through the soil. The beige, crinkled shells hold up to four nuts, each encased in a pink, or brown, brittle papery skin. The nuts are sold in the shell; shelled and raw; roasted and salted or 'dry-roasted' with a barbecue flavouring. They are high in protein (up to 28 per cent) and in fat (almost 50 per cent). Mainly used as a snack, especially with drinks, they can also be crushed or ground to flavour bread, cakes and biscuits/cookies and to make a creamy soup. Whole nuts are good in salads, with shredded red or white cabbage, and in casseroles.

Peanut butter Dr J. H. Kellogg, brother of the food industrialist, was famous not only for his cornflakes. He also invented peanut butter to add variety to the vegetarian diet of his patients at his Battle Creek sanatorium in Michigan. The 'butter' is made by grinding roasted, unsalted nuts and mixing them with a little oil. It is sold in jars and tubs and available in smooth

and crunchy textures. To make your own, see page 37. Use as a sandwich or cake spread; in cakes, bread, biscuits/cookies and teabreads.

Peanut, arachide or **groundnut oil** The oil contains 30 per cent polyunsaturated linoleic acid. The unrefined oil has a pronounced nutty flavour; refined types are practically tasteless. Use in salad dressings; in cakes; or for all types of frying.

Pear, dried Halved dried pears are sold separately, or in a selection of mixed tree fruits (see pages 8–9). Soak them in water or fruit juice – cloudy apple juice is ideal – and poach in the soaking liquid for 20–30 minutes. Use in a compote of dried pears spiced with cinnamon or cloves; as a cooked pear purée mixed with yoghurt or cream for fruit fool, ice cream and mousse. Serve pear sauce with sliced fresh pears.

Pearl barley Not a health food at all, pearl barley is the polished barley grain, with the bran and germ removed – the equivalent of white rice. It is used in casseroles for thickening and to add starch and bulk.

Pecan Native to the southern USA, pecan nuts can rightly be described as the all-American nut. They have smooth, shiny, oval skins which can be vivid pinkish-red and kernels resembling walnuts. They are sold in shell, or shelled and halved or broken. Apart from in pecan pie, with its sticky toffee filling, pecans can be used in salads; in confectionery; as cake and pudding decoration; chopped in cakes, biscuits/cookies and teabread; as a snack, with raisins or muscatels; or with cheese.

Phosphorus Together with calcium, phosphorus is one of the major mineral elements required for healthy bones. On average, nearly 1 kg (2¼ lb) of bone weight is phosphorus. It is found in the form of phosphates in whole-grain cereals and soya products especially.

Pigeon pea, see *gungo pea*

Pine nut The edible seeds or kernels of the cone of some pine trees native to the south-western USA, they are small, oblong and milky-white in colour and creamy in flavour. Pine nuts are significantly more expensive than many other nuts and are therefore used in small quantites; in salads; in stuffings for vegetables and classic Italian veal rolls, with cheese and mushrooms; or as garnish, especially for steamed and stir-fried vegetables.

Pinto bean An export of the USA, pinto beans are a type of kidney bean, pink with brown speckles. Pre-soak, then cook in boiling, unsalted water for 2–2½ hours. Use in salads; for a savoury hummus-type paste; tossed with rice; as a garnish for meat casserole; in soups.

Pistachio The fruit of a deciduous tree native to the Middle East, pistachios, a highly profitable crop, are now cultivated in the USA, the Mediterranean and Mexico. The nuts have beigey-brown hard shells which burst open to reveal the bright green and vivid pink kernels. They are sold in shell, shelled, and salted. Use as a snack; in ice cream; in vegetable and herb pâté; to garnish egg dishes; in stuffings.

Polenta, see *cornmeal*

Pollen tablets The tablets are an extract of pollen, taken as a rapid source of energy to relieve tiredness.

Polyunsaturated fats Most vegetable oils have a high proportion of these fatty acids, which have carbon atoms joined together by two or more double bonds. The acids are liquid at room temperature and are thought to have at least an unharmful effect on blood cholesterol level; there are claims that they actually lower that level.

Different vegetable oils have varying compositions of these fats. The polyunsaturated fatty acid linoleic acid, present in all vegetable oils, is particularly high in soya, safflower and sunflower oil and the margarine made with sunflower oil. This acid cannot be synthesized in the body and is known as an essential acid. Linolenic acid [sic] is present in many vegetable oils, and arachidonic acid is present in unsaturated animal fats, especially liver and eggs. See entries for mono-unsaturated fats and unsaturated fats.

Popcorn A variety of corn, or maize, that 'explodes' on contact with heat. In the USA, where snacking popcorn is a favourite pastime, there are electric heat-controlled popcorn poppers. A large pan serves just as well. Heat 30 ml (2 tablespoons) oil, spoon in popcorn to cover the base in a single layer, put on the lid (very important) and shake the pan over moderate heat. As the kernels explode they will rise to the top and make way for late poppers. Toss popped corn in melted butter and honey, maple syrup, or salt and barbecue seasoning, as desired.

Poppy seed The minute round seeds can be bluish-black (the type used to decorate traditional Jewish and Central European baked goods) or cream (the variety used in Indian dishes). Both are sold whole or ground and are slightly spicy. It is best to buy them whole, then crush them to use in bread, cakes and biscuits/cookies. Use the whole seeds to sprinkle *on* bread, cakes and biscuits/cookies. Toss whole seeds with buttered noodles.

Porridge oats 'Quick' porridge oats are whole oats rolled, partially cooked, cooled and dried. They are similar in appearance to oat flakes or rolled oats and can be used in the same way (see above).

Potato flour This brilliant white, very finely ground flour is made from cooked and dried potatoes. It can be mixed in small quantities with other flours in bread, and especially (in the proportion 1 to 4) in shortbread. It can be used, as cornflour/cornstarch is, to thicken sauces and soup.

Pot cheese, see *curd cheese*

Propolis Nothing in a beehive is wasted! Propolis is the substance which bees use as an adhesive. They inject it with antibiotics and enzymes. It is sold in tablet form and as a liquid.

Protein Proteins are necessary for body-building and maintenance and to provide energy. On average, proteins consumed in the Western diet are obtained 60 per cent from animal products, 30 per cent from cereals and cereal products and 10 per cent from fruit and vegetables. The consumed protein is broken down in the body into the various amino acids and recreated as body protein, which can only be produced if all the essential amino acids are available at the same time – that is, eaten at the same meal. Meat, fish, eggs and milk are first-class (complete) proteins. Wholemeal bread lacks one of the acids found in pulses, while baked beans on toast makes the perfect protein combination; the American dish of succotash, corn and beans is another.

Prune These shiny-black dried fruits are the 'plums' of old-fashioned plum cakes and puddings. Lower in calories than most other dried fruits, they are dried from extra-sweet varieties of plum taken to the USA by early immigrants from Europe. They are sold whole both with and without stones, canned in syrup, and in the form of freeze-dried flakes, a purplish-black coarse powder. Use stoned whole fruit raw as a sweetmeat, filled with apricot or almond paste, soft cheese, or whole nuts; added to casseroles especially of beef and pork; chopped in stuffings for meat and poultry; in cakes, bread and puddings. Stewed prunes, lightly spiced with cinnamon, are a traditional breakfast dish. Prune flakes are good in muesli, cake mixtures and milk puddings.

Pulses The dried seeds of leguminous plants, from broad beans to chick peas, flageolets to lentils, are known as pulses. They are all very high in protein and so an important ingredient especially in a vegetarian diet and in fibre. See separate entries.

Pumpkin seed The flat, oval seeds have very tough and teeth-resistant outer husks. Once these are removed, the shiny green seeds are almost silky. They are sold both whole and 'shelled'. Use as a snack; in salads and muesli; or as a garnish, especially for soups, casseroles, meat dishes and curries.

Quark A firm, smooth low-fat soft cheese of German origin, with only about 168 calories per 100 g (4 oz) (½ cup). Use as cream cheese, in sandwiches; mixed with fruit purée or grated rind as cake filling and decoration; to fill salad vegetables for canapés; in salads; as a flan filling, topped with fruit or cooked vegetables.

Raisin The fruit of the vine, raisins are dried from grapes and exported from California, South Africa, Iran and Afghanistan. According to the variety of grape, raisins vary in size, from

mid-brown to almost black in colour, and some, the most suitable for cooking, are seedless. Use as a snack, especially with nuts; in salads, especially with shredded red or white cabbage; in baking; with ham and pork dishes; as sauce with meat, fish and puddings; in ice cream; as pie filling. For extra flavour pre-soak in fruit juice, wine or liqueur. See also *muscatel*.

Red kidney or **chilli bean** Indigenous to the New World, dried red kidney beans are best known in 'chilli con carne', a highly spiced Mexican dish. They are medium-sized, oval and dark red verging sometimes on purple. They can be bought dried, or cooked and canned. To cook, pre-soak, then – a word of warning – fast-boil the beans for at least 12 minutes to drive off toxins. Continue cooking in boiling, unsalted water for 1–1¼ hours. Use with tomato sauce as accompaniment; in soups, salads and casseroles, specially with pork and beef; as a hot or cold purée; tossed with rice; in vegetable hotpots, pies and pasties.

Rice There are many thousands of varieties of rice, which can be divided into long-, medium- and short-grain types. The grains are encased in a tough outer husk which has to be removed. Brown rice is the whole grain minus the husk. White rice is the 'shelled' grain minus most of the fat, minerals, much of the protein and the vitamin thiamine (B1). (Deficiency in thiamine causes beri-beri.) In India much of the rice crop is par-boiled in a way which transfers this and other vitamins and minerals into the endosperm; so all is not lost.

Both patna and basmati are varieties of long-grained milled white rice which are readily cooked with well-separated grains.

Rice flour Flour is made both from brown and from the by-products of milled white rice; it includes the bran and is rich in B vitamins. It has a low gluten content and should be mixed with high-gluten flour for leavened breads. A little (in the proportion of 1 part to 4) improves the texture of shortbread. It is good for thickening and in batters.

Rice, wild A staple food of the North American Indians, wild rice is in fact an aquatic grass that yields long, thin almost black grains. It is now grown commercially in man-made swamps. It is so very expensive that great care must be taken in cooking – it readily goes soggy. To cook, simmer in 1½ times its volume of water (1 cup rice to 1½ cups water) for 15–20 minutes. Add salt and leave to rest in a warm place for 5 minutes. Serve as a 'vegetable' accompaniment tossed with chopped herbs and butter.

Roasted wheat, see *bulghar*

Rock salt, see *salt*

Rolled oats, see *oat flakes*

Rose cocoa bean, see *borlotti bean*

Roseship syrup A good source of vitamin C, rosehip syrup is made from the fruits of the wild dog rose. It can be diluted as a nutritious (but rather sticky) drink and is good with sparkling mineral water. Use to sweeten and flavour syrup for fruit salad; in milk puddings; in confectionery.

Rosewater Made from the extract of rose petals, this highly aromatic water is used extensively in Middle Eastern and Indian cookery to flavour desserts. It is also available as triple-strength rosewater, in which form a few drops will flavour 300 ml (½ pint) (1¼ cups) syrup or custard. Use in syrup for fresh and dried fruit salad; in ice cream, sorbets and milk puddings, including rice and semolina; in confectionery.

Royal jelly Bees make this jelly, which is like honey, to feed their queen. Rich in enzymes and natural hormones, it is available in tablet form.

Rye A staple crop of Eastern and Northern European countries until more hardy varieties of wheat were raised, rye gives a strong, bitter and rather acidic flavour to bread, which can be brown, grey or black. The grains can be cooked and served as wheat. Quicker-cooking cracked rye grains are also sold. Cook whole grains in boiling water for 1¼ hours, cracked rye for 15 minutes. Both are good as accompaniment, or, as risotto, with herbs, meat or vegetables. Cracked rye is good as a bread and scone topping, and can be added in small quantities to bread, scone, pastry and crumble dough.

Rye flakes Rolled rye grains, or rye flakes, can be used as other flaked cereals. In porridge, muesli, flapjacks, treacle tart, pastry dough, cakes, bread and toppings.

Rye flour Most recipes for rye bread call for a half-and-half mixture of rye and wholewheat flour. All-rye bread such as pumpernickel is flat and heavy, due to the low gluten content of the flour – but very tasty. Rye bread is especially good with cream or cottage cheese, sour pickles, continental sausages or smoked ham, and for open sandwiches. Finger-sized strips of rye bread are good for dips.

Safflower oil The oil is pressed from the seed of a member of the *Compositae* plant family, indigenous to the regions of the Nile and now cultivated in the Middle East and North Africa. It has a linoleic acid content – that is to say of the 'good' polyunsaturated fatty acids – of over 60 per cent. It is widely used in the USA. Use for salad dressing and as a frying and cooking medium.

Sake Japanese rice wine, extensively used in sauces. Dry sherry is not so much a substitute, more a completely different alternative.

Salt Salt, or sodium chloride, is an essential mineral. Its role is to balance the body fluids. In a completely salt-free diet (if that were possible) the body would become dehydrated. Sodium chloride is present to a greater or lesser extent in all foods; the level in animal products and especially in smoked meats

and fish is particularly high. It is an ancient and effective preservative and is used to draw out the liquid in foods – as in aubergine/eggplant before cooking. 'Dégorging' with salt draws out the bitter juices. Salt is definitely not wanted for cooking dried pulses; the addition of salt to the water prevents them from absorbing the liquid and becoming rehydrated and tender.

Sea salt, or bay salt as the crude form is known, is obtained by evaporating sea water. In the process the substance is purified to remove harmful elements. In Britain sea salt is produced only in Maldon, in Essex, on the east coast.

Kitchen salt, or block salt, is obtained by pumping water into salt-bearing underground rock layers. The brine is concentrated by evaporation until the salt crystallizes and is at the same time partly purified. It is sold in varying grades of coarseness, in block form and as tablets. These are taken to keep up the salt level in very hot climates. Rock salt is a less refined type of kitchen salt, with larger crystals.

Table salt is 'land' salt which has been finely ground. The moisture-attracting salts are removed (leaving the salt with more pure sodium content) and substances such as starch and phosphate of lime added to make it flow easily.

Iodized salt has potassium added to free-running table salt.

Samosa Health-food shops which sell ready-to-eat foods and lunch-time snacks usually include samosas. They are small pastry triangles filled with spiced meat and vegetable mixtures and deep-fried in oil – the Indian equivalent of meat and vegetable pasties. See page 56.

Saturated fats Saturated fatty acids are the ones that set hard at room temperature and are mainly of animal origin. They are found in butter, lard, dripping, suet, hard margarines and the visible and invisible fat on meat. They are also present to a high degree in dairy products – milk, full-fat cheeses and cream – and in coconut. These are the fats that are considered to contribute to heart disease.

Semolina Wholewheat semolina is coarsely ground from hard, durum wheat and has 13.5 per cent protein and 10 per cent dietary fibre. For milk pudding, stir 100 g (4 oz) (⅔ cup) semolina into 600 ml (1 pint) (2½ cups) milk, bring to the boil and simmer for 3 minutes, stirring constantly. Beat in up to 100 g (4 oz) (¾ cup) dried fruits, 5 ml (1 teaspoon) ground cinnamon and 2 beaten eggs. Bake is a greased dish in the oven at 180°C, 350°F, Gas 4 for 25 minutes. Serve topped with yoghurt and honey. For salad, stir dry semolina into oil and lemon dressing, soak for 30 minutes then stir in chopped onion, herbs, sliced tomatoes. Use semolina as a high-fibre thickening for sauces, soups, stews, casseroles and to absorb fruit juice in pies to prevent soggy pastry.

Sesame oil The oil pressed from

sesame seeds is widely used in the Far East. It has little taste – certainly no hint of the spiciness of the seed – and remains fresh and stable almost indefinitely in any climate. It has a polyunsaturated rating of 40 per cent linoleic acid, with 50 per cent unsaturated oleic acid. Use in salad dressings and as cooking medium.

Sesame seed Throughout the East sesame seeds, blessed in Hindu mythology by the god Yama, are a symbol of immortality. The spice seeds are small, flat and egg-shaped and can be cream or black. The raw seeds are mild in flavour but develop a nutty taste when they are roasted. The ground seeds can be used to make the Indian sweetmeat halva, and are the main ingredient in the Arab and Turkish speciality tahina paste (see separate entry). Use in salad dressings, sprinkled on salads, especially combined with fruit such as sliced apple; in fruit salads; sprinkled on bread, cakes and biscuits/cookies; in muesli; in bread and teabread; to coat balls of cream cheese for cocktail appetizers; to garnish soup and savoury dips. To toast them, spread on a baking tray and cook at 180°C, 350°F, Gas 4 for 20 minutes, or under a medium grill for 10 minutes. Stir often.

Shirataki noodles Made from vegetable starch derived from the tubes of the 'devil's tongue plant', a member of the arum family. The noodles feature in the Japanese dish sukiyaki (see page 97). They are sometimes descriptively called white waterfall noodles.

Shiro-miso A white soya-bean paste used as a flavouring, thickener and source of protein in Japanese cookery.

Shoyu Type of soy sauce. See page 98.

Skimmed milk, see *milk*

Sodium Most commonly occurring in common salt, with chloride, sodium is an elementary alkaline metal forming the basis of soda.

Soft margarine, see *margarine*

Sorghum, or kafir Indigenous to Africa and India, sorghum is a tough grain which resists the severest drought conditions. It is a type of millet which can be cooked and served as whole wheat or barley. Sorghum flour is gluten-free and therefore makes hard, flat bread unless mixed with a high-gluten meal. Store under refrigeration, otherwise the oil in the germ goes rancid.

Soya bean Native to China, the beans are also cultivated in Japan, Korea and the USA. They contain all 8 essential amino acids which the body cannot manufacture, and so are the only first-class protein plant food. As such, they are an important protein derivative in the Third World, not only as dried legumes, but in a range of products including soya paste, soya milk and textured vegetable protein or TVP (see separate entries).

The fat in the beans is unsaturated and they are rich in most minerals and vitamins. Additionally, they contain iron in a form which can be easily assimilated.

For all these 'plus' points, the small, almost round, white beans lack both flavour and character. A spicy sauce or the accompaniment of crisp, colourful vegetables is almost essential. To cook, pre-soak, then cook in boiling, unsalted water for up to 3½ hours to soften. As with all pulses, pressure-cooking at high pressure cuts cooking time considerably. Use as a vegetable, with an interesting sauce; in salads, with flavouring herbs, in soups, casseroles and stews; as hot or cold spiced purée.

Soya flour The flour contains no gluten but can be added to wheat flour for extra protein in the ratio 1 to 8. It is sold in 3 types – 'full-fat' soya flour has 20 per cent fat; 'medium-fat' has 5–8 per cent, and there is also a fat-free version. The lower the fat content, the more liquid will be needed to form a pliable dough. Use in small quantities in bread; to thicken sauces, soups and casseroles; and in salad dressing.

Soya grits The long cooking time for soya beans can be a handicap – in which case, use the grits. They are made from cooked and dried beans crushed to granules. (Soya splits are slightly larger.) No pre-soaking is required. Cook in twice volume of water or stock (1 cup grits or splits to 2 cups liquid) for 45 minutes. Use as an accompaniment, or, with added vegetables, as 'risotto'; or dry and form into a paste, add spice, shape into croquettes and fry.

Soya milk The milk, which is somewhat similar to skimmed milk, is sold in cans, bottles and as a spray-dried powder. It is useful not only for vegans but for those allergic to cow's milk, and is easy to digest. Soya milk has more iron than cow's milk but less calcium. Use as regular milk.

Soya oil, or **soya bean oil** Both unrefined and refined soya oil are available. The unrefined oil is, of course, the natural product. It has a strong flavour and aroma and a deep amber colour, whereas the processed oil is pale corn-coloured and almost tasteless. The oil is high in polyunsaturates, containing 60 per cent linoleic acid. Use in salad and as a frying medium.

Soya paste, or **miso** The paste is made from whole, fermented beans; some types have added salt and barley or rice grains which affect both strength of flavour and colour. It is sold in tough plastic bags. Snip off the corner and squeeze the paste into a lidded jar. Use as yeast extract, as a last-minute flavouring addition to soup, vegetable casseroles, stews; in marinades and for vegetable pickle.

Soy sauce A familiar condiment on the tables of Chinese restaurants, soy sauce is a strongly flavoured soya-bean preparation with a high salt content. For uses, see pages 98–9.

Split pea A variety of legume grown specially for drying, split peas can be yellow, green or pale orange. In the drying process the skin comes off and the seeds split in half. To cook, pre-soak, then cook in boiling, unsalted water for about 1 hour. They were used traditionally in pease pudding (the pulses used to be boiled in a cloth immersed in bacon stock). Use for soups; in casseroles; or puréed, to thicken sauces, or cooked until dry and shaped into 'cakes' for frying or baking.

Sprouting seeds Dried bean and pea seeds and whole grains can be sprouted to make crisp, crunchy, salad shoots that can be quickly and lightly cooked by stir-frying, steaming or simmering. Mung beans are the ones which produce the familiar Chinese bean shoots, or bean sprouts. Try fenugreek, aduki, alfalfa, lentils, chick peas, soya and haricot beans among the pulses.

Sprouting grains are just as successful: try oats, wheat, barley, corn and rye. Soak the grains in warm water overnight to soften them. See page 40 for method. Grains take up to 5 days to sprout.

Sprouting seeds are rich in vitamins, especially vitamin C, and proteins.

Stabilized yoghurt Home-made yoghurt has countless uses in cooking. When stirred into sauces or casseroles, or boiled, yoghurt sometimes separates: to avoid this, stabilize it first. Mix 15 ml (1 tablespoon) flour or cornflour/cornstarch to a paste with water, gradually stir in 600 ml (1 pint) (2½ cups) yoghurt and bring to the boil, stirring constantly. Simmer very gently for 10 minutes. Use at once or cool and store in the refrigerator in a covered container.

Stabilized yoghurt is not suitable for use to make the next batch. The culture is killed by the boiling.

Sucrose Sucrose is the sugar obtained from sugar cane and sugar beet. It is also obtained – by bees – from the nectar of flowers, which is mainly sucrose. This is converted by the bee into fructose and glucose, known as 'invert' sugar.

Sultana This dried vine fruit is produced from white grapes grown in the USA, Turkey, Greece, Australia and South Africa. UK food regulations permit the addition of a small quantity of sulphur dioxide to preserve the colour and a fine film of sprayed oil to keep the fruits from sticking. Check the label if you wish to avoid additives. Sultanas have 7 per cent dietary fibre and are 64.7 per cent sugar. They are a rich source of vitamins, especially vitamin B, and minerals, especially iron and potassium. Use raw in muesli, salads and as a snack with nuts. In cakes, bread, scones, biscuits/cookies, pastries, curry and rice dishes as a garnish to meat and vegetable dishes.

Sunflower oil Almost half the weight of sunflower seeds is oil, made up of over 60 per cent polyunsaturated linoleic acids as well as oleic and palmitic oils. It is a good source of vitamins E, A and D. Use in salads and as a cooking medium.

Sunflower seed The USA and USSR are the main sources of this nutritionally important crop. The seeds, apart from their high oil content, are rich in B-complex vitamins, phosphorus, magnesium, iron, calcium, potassium, proteins and vitamin E. They also contain a number of trace elements. The hulled, grey, oval seeds, which taste almost creamy, are sold raw, toasted, and toasted and salted. Use raw as a snack, in muesli, salads, as a garnish for vegetables such as broccoli and cauliflower; in fillings for vegetables, stuffings for meat and poultry; or as a crunchy topping for bread and cakes. Toast the seeds (as for sesame seeds) for extra flavour. You can also buy sunflower meal, from the residue of the seeds after the oil is pressed out.

Sweetcorn, see *corn*

Tabasco This hot, fiery red sauce sold in small, slender bottles – a little goes a long way – is made from hot red peppers matured for 3 years in salt and mixed with vinegar. It is used in Creole and Latin American cookery. A few drops pep up sauces, especially tomato, soups, especially crab and gumbo, and casseroles, especially fish and shellfish. Tabasco is also used – sparingly – as a condiment; good with egg and rice dishes.

Tahina, or **tahini** Whole sesame seeds ground to a creamy paste, tahina has a consistency rather similar to that of peanut butter. It is an optional ingredient in chick-pea paste (hummus). It can be used to thicken sauces, soups and casseroles and as a sandwich spread seasoned with either soya sauce or honey.

Tamari sauce This Japanese soy sauce, made from whole fermented soya beans and sea salt, has a less raw and harsh flavour than other types. To use, add about 15 ml (1 tablespoon) to meat or mixed vegetable soups (not those with a subtle, creamy flavour) and to casseroles. Add a few drops of sauce to the water or stock when cooking rice and other grains and to salad dressing. Also, use as a condiment.

Tamarind The flavouring comes from the pods of a tree that grows wild in India and is cultivated throughout the tropics; it is sometimes called the Indian date. The 20-cm (8-inch)-long dark brown pods are seeded and partly dried and compressed into a sticky block which keeps almost indefinitely. The pulp contains about 12 per cent tartaric acid and so is very bitter. To use, soak the pulp in hot water, then squeeze out the juice. It is used to give a sour flavour to curries and is much stronger than, say, lime juice.

Tempeh A fermented bean cake made in Indonesia by inoculating cooked soya beans with a bacterial culture.

Textured vegetable protein (TVP) Owing to the world protein shortage and forecasts that this situation can only worsen, major industrial concerns are experimenting with non-animal proteins. At present these are largely marketed as 'meat substitutes' or 'meat extenders' and have not found a place in family menus on their own merits. One type of TVP is made from soya-flour dough heated, extruded through a nozzle under pressure, dried and cut into pieces. Another is made from soya protein concentrate spun into threads, with added colour and flavouring. TVP is sold frozen, canned or fried and in packets, in the form of chunks, grits and granules. Cook according to the directions on the packet in tomato sauce to serve with pasta; in pies and pasties. It needs plenty of additional flavour!

Tiger nut The rhizomes of *Cyperus esculenta*, a plant native to Africa, tiger nuts (which are not nuts at all) are sold dried. They are mid-brown, shrivelled and the size of sultanas. They are eaten raw as a very chewy snack. Some actually taste of the milkiness of nuts, others – a rare bonus – have the sweetness of dried fruits. In Africa they are ground into starchy flour.

Tisanes, or herbal teas For centuries herbal teas have been taken as preventatives and cures, and each of the early civilizations recorded recognition of their powers. Now most people who drink tisanes do so because they are refreshing, pleasant and soothing. Health-food shops have come up to date and sell a range of attractively packaged herbal tea-bags. Lime flowers, dandelion, comfrey, borage, mint, camomile, hibiscus flowers, sarsaparilla, peppermint . . . take your choice. See also page 79.

Tofu A soya-bean product of infinite variety and usefulness, *tofu*, the Japanese name for beancurd, is made from soya milk coagulated with lactone and calcium chloride and sold loose ('wet'), or in cartons, or in cans. The blocks are creamy-white and soft but solid – like very thick blancmange. There are two kinds, cotton and silk. In the carton, imported long-life silk beancurd from Japan keeps fresh without refrigeration for up to 6 months. *Tofu* can be sliced and fried, or tossed in crumbs and deep-fried, served as a salad (perhaps instead of cream cheese), mashed and flavoured for a sweet or savoury dip, or made into a creamy soup with vegetables – the cans and cartons offer many ideas and full instructions. It can of course also be used in many Chinese and Japanese dishes.

Trace elements, see *minerals*

Triticale The grain is a hybrid, a cross between wheat and rye which has a higher protein content than either. Another advantage is that the grain contains lysine, an essential amino acid low in wheat. Triticale is cultivated in the northern USA, Canada and the USSR, and to a small extent in the UK. The flour has a low gluten content and makes a soft, delicate dough. The grains can be used for sprouting (see sprouting seeds).

Turtle bean, see *black bean*

TVP, see *textured vegetable protein*

UHT milk, see *milk*

Unsaturated fats There are over 40 fatty acids found in animal and vegetable foods. Those with less than a full quota of hydrogen atoms, and which are liquid at room temperature, are termed unsaturated fats. See *mono-unsaturated fats* and *polyunsaturated fats*.

Urd bean Widely grown throughout India and the Far East, the dried beans have dull, black skins and are related to mung beans. They are sold whole, skinned and split, and are widely used in Indian cooking in soups and as a purée.

Vinegar Its name is an adequate description – *vin aigre* means sour wine in French. Before the wine-making process was properly understood, the last of the summer wine turned sour, to vinegar, long before the next harvest. Vinegar is fermented from yeast cells in the air which turn sugar into alcohol, and from natural vinegar yeasts which convert the alcohol into acetic acid. The acetic acid content varies, and is subject to regulation. In both Britain and the USA this acid level must be a minimum 4 per cent for malt and cider vinegar, and 6 per cent for wine vinegars.

Malt vinegar is made from malted barley. After maturing, it is given its characteristic brown colour by the addition of caramel. It is used for pickling and whenever subtlety of flavour is not important.

Distilled vinegar is usually made from vinegar. It is clear and colourless and has a stronger flavour.

Cider vinegar (q.v.) is made from apple pulp and is good in salads, cooking and even as a health drink. Wine vinegars made from red and white wines are good for salad dressings and sauces.

Flavoured vinegars infused with herbs, spices or leaves, such as tarragon vinegar, are easy to make at home. See page 100.

Vitamins Vitamins are organic substances needed by the body though in small amounts. Vitamin A (found in liver, butter and converted from the carotene in vegetables) is needed for sight, the skin, the throat and the bronchial tubes.

The complex group of B vitamins releases energy, derived from carbohydrates, fats and proteins, and makes red cells in the blood. B vitamins are found in liver, kidney, meat, milk, fish, cereals, nuts, eggs and fresh vegetables. Cooking destroys much of the thiamine, vitamin B1, which is particularly high in potatoes.

Vitamin C, ascorbic acid, from soft and citrus fruits and many types of vegetables, is needed to make tissue that binds the body cells. Again, much of the vitamin is lost in cooking, and also on exposure to air.

Vitamin D, from dairy products and fish oils, is needed for bones and teeth, to control the absorption of calcium from the digestive system and its excretion from the body by the absorption of sunlight through the skin.

Vitamin E, found in wheatgerm and the germ of other grains, in fats and vegetables, is necessary, but its functions are not yet clearly understood.

Vitamin K, present in leafy vegetables and manufactured in the intestine, is needed for the blood.

Many vitamin pills or supplements are available; however, medical experts generally agree that given a healthy diet none of them is necessary.

Wakame A type of seaweed which is sold in sprouts or bunches.

Walnut From the large, beautiful *Juglans regia* and *Juglans nigra* trees, walnuts have smooth, green outer husks covering dull pale brown shells. The kernels inside split into two halves when they are released. They are sold in shell, in halves and, more cheaply for cooking, in pieces. Use in salads, muesli, chopped in cakes; as a decoration on cakes and puddings; in soups; in casseroles, especially with chicken or beef. The young unripe nuts can be pickled in the husks (and then turn black), to serve with cheese and meats or make into chutney. See pages 28–9.

Walnut oil Walnuts contain some 60 per cent oil, which is a speciality of French growers. It is high in iodine and has a superb flavour, which is particularly good in salads. The oil is sold in cans or bottles and once opened has a short shelf-life. Use within 2–3 months.

Wheat Wheat is the major staple food of the world and varieties have been bred that can grow in almost every combination of soil and climatic condition. Wheat is sold as whole grains, which can be cooked and served as rice, as rolled flakes; coarsely ground cracked wheat and roasted and cracked grains, burghul. The flour ground from the whole wheat is extremely nutritious and higher in gluten than any other flour. See separate entries, and pages 59–60.

Wheat flakes The whole wheat grains are rolled to produce flakes which cook more quickly than the grains, and can be eaten raw in muesli. Cook in twice their volume of water (1 cup of wheat flakes to 2 cups water) for 10–12 minutes. Use as porridge, with yoghurt or honey. Sprinkle raw flakes on bread and scone dough; stir in small amounts into bread, scone pastry and cake mixtures.

Wheatgerm, see *germ*

Wheatgerm oil The germ, or kernel, of the whole wheat grain has a high fat content. This is extracted as oil, and sold in health-food shops as a dietary supplement.

Wheatmeal flour This is the most confusing term of all. It means that the flour – or the bread made from it – is made from wheat. It does not say and does not mean that it is made from the whole wheat, including the germ and the bran. The flour may indeed be milled white (wheat) flour coloured with additives to make it brown. If a percentage figure is stated, such as 85 per cent or 81 per cent, this means that 15 and 19 per cent respectively of the germ and bran have been extracted (this is known as the extraction rate).

Wholewheat or wholemeal flour The flour is ground from the whole wheat grain and includes the nutritious germ and the higher-fibre bran. It is sold both plain and with sifted-in raising agents, as self-raising flour. Wholewheat flour makes a closer-textured loaf and a slightly heavier pastry than white flour. The pastry has a 'natural', almost nutty flavour which blends well with both sweet and savoury fillings (see pages 57 and 59–60).

Wild rice, see *rice, wild*

Yeast Yeast has been used as a leavening agent for dough for thousands of years. It is a living organism which multiplies on sugar liquids in warm conditions. As it develops it produces carbon dioxide. It is these gas bubbles which expand to aerate and raise the dough.

Baker's yeast, which is high in vitamin B, is available in fresh and dried form. Fresh yeast should be a light beige colour, soft and moist. It works best at a temperature of 25 °C, 78 °F. Dried yeast is made in two types, one which is sprinkled on to warm liquid ingredients and acts most quickly at 40 °C, 104 °F, and the other, 'easy-blend', type, which is stirred into the dry ingredients.

Brewer's yeast is rich in protein, minerals and the B vitamins thiamine, niacin and riboflavin. It is available in powdered form and can be taken in drinks or sprinkled on cereals.

Yeast extract The more nutritious brewer's yeast (see previous entry) is used to make yeast extract, a sticky brown substance with a salty flavour. The extract can be used as a spread; to flavour soup and stock and the liquid in which rice and other grains are cooked; or as a hot drink.

Yoghurt Yoghurt can be made from any type of milk – cow's milk, goat's milk, ewe's milk and powdered types – by the introduction of a living culture which sets the milk into a semi-solid and adds acidity. Many claims are made for its properties, including the main one of longevity. A substantiated fact is that the introduced bacteria in the yoghurt, *Lactobacillus bulgaricus* and *Streptococcus thermophilus*, serve to deter harmful bacteria building up in the intestine.

Home-made yoghurt needs stabilizing before use in cooking, or it may separate. See pages 84–5. Note that commercial fruit yoghurts have a high sugar content, and are far from being health-foods.

Yoghurt cheese By straining yoghurt to separate the curds and whey you can make a delicious soft, unripened cheese. See page 85.

RECIPE INDEX

Almond comfort   87
Apple rings in apricot
    sauce   11
Apricot ice shaker   83
Apricot mousse   11
Apricot paste   11
Apricot sorbet   93
Aubergines/egg-plants with
    chestnut filling   35

Baked apples with figs   21
Baked New York
    cheesecake   15
Banana and walnut
    teabread   23
Banana magic   83
Barley vegetable pilaff   67
Bean-bag
    courgettes/zucchini   45
Borscht   88
Boston baked beans   51
Brazil-nut toffee   31
Buckwheat blinis   71
Buckwheat spaghetti with
    prawn sauce   75
Bulghar salad   61

Candied orange peel cake   25
Cashew-nut griddle scones   35
Cassoulet   50
Celebration cake   17
Chapattis   55
Chick-pea paste
    (hummus)   44
Chilli beans   50
Coconut meringue pie   39
Cornbread   63
Cous-cous   71
Crème fraîche   93

Dairy salad   89
Dal   55
Date 'sugar'   21
Devils on horseback   13
Dried fruit compote   9
Dried fruit noodles   77

Fig brûlée   92
Fish and corn chowder   63
Flageolets with garlic   53
Fresh-fruit muesli   87
Fruit, vegetable, nut and rice
    salad   69

Garden salad with
    almonds   27
Granola   65

Halva with pistachios   39
Haricot bean chowder   47
Hazelnut meringue
    baskets   31
Hummus (chick-pea
    paste)   44
Hungarian-style pancakes   16

Lamb polo   69
Lasagne verdi with lentil
    sauce   77
Lentil and tomato
    pasties/pie   56
Liquid gold   82
Love-apple pick-me-up   80

Macerated fruits   8
Matsutake gohan (rice with
    mushrooms)   96
Minestrone soup   46
Mint and pistachio ice
    cream   38
Miso vegetable soup   99
Moors and Christians   53
Muesli   65
Muscatels in brandy   19
Mushroom and pepper
    pizza   60

Nut and seed loaf   41

Oatcakes   65
Orange barley water   80
Orange yoghurt   87
Orchard blossom   82

Pasta and Roquefort salad   74
Peach nectar   81
Peach reveille   12
Peanut bread   37
Peanut butter   37
Peanut butter cookies   37
Pease pudding   52
Pecan pie   33
Pitta   45
Porridge   64
Potato and sultana salad   15
Prune dominoes   13
Purple sunset   81

Rice with mushrooms
    (matsutake gohan)   96
Roast and salted chestnuts   35
Roast sweetcorn   63
Roquefort and walnut
    mousse   29
Rose petal wonder   83
Rye baps   67

Salade niçoise   49
Salted almonds   27
Samosas   56
Seaweed salad   94
Skewered meatballs   19
Spinach and pasta moulds   74
Split-pea soup   47
Steamed dumplings   95
Stir-fried mushrooms and
    legumes   95
Stuffed mushrooms   97
Sukiyaki   97

Tandoori chicken   90
Three-bean salad   49
Tisanes   79
Tomato sauce   75
Tropical salad   22
Trout with almonds   27
Turkey and pine nut rolls   33
Turkish pilaff   19
Tuscany lamb   76
Tutti-frutti ice cream   25
Tzajiki   91

Vegetable curry   54

Walnut soup   29
Wheatgerm bread   61

Yoghurt   84
Yoghurt cheese   85
Yoghurt cheese and walnut
    worlds   89
Yoghurt dawn   86
Yoghurt salad (tzajiki)   91